AUTOBIOGRAPHY
OF
ANTON RUBINSTEIN.

AUTOBIOGRAPHY

OF

ANTON RUBINSTEIN

1829–1889

TRANSLATED FROM THE RUSSIAN

BY ALINE DELANO

BOSTON
LITTLE, BROWN, AND COMPANY
1890

Republished, 1970
Scholarly Press, 22929 Industrial Drive East
St. Clair Shores, Michigan 48080

Library of Congress Catalog Card Number: 70-131820
Standard Book Number 403-00707-0

Copyright, 1890,
BY LITTLE, BROWN, AND COMPANY.

Rubinstein, Anton, 1829–1894.
　Autobiography. Translated from the Russian by Aline Delano. St. Clair Shores, Mich., Scholarly Press, 1970.
　　xii, 171 p. 21 cm.

Translation of Автобіографическія воспоминанія (romanized: Avtobiograficheskiﬁa vospominaniﬁa)
　Reprint of the 1890 ed.
　"Supplement: Rubinstein as a composer (p. [141]–163); Rubinstein as a pianist (p. 163–171)"

ML410.R89A32　　1970　　　780'.924　[B]　　　70–131820
ISBN 0-403-00707-0　　　　　　　　　　　　　　　MARC

Library of Congress　　　70 [4]　　　　　　　MN

PREFACE.

ON the 18th of November, 1889, Russia celebrated the Jubilee of her greatest living pianist and composer, Anton Rubinstein. Although from time to time various articles and criticisms on the life and works of the famous musician have been published, the biographical details, often inaccurate, possessed little or no value. It is a well-known fact that Rubinstein has always shown a reluctance to talk about himself or about his musical career. The idea suggested itself that it would be well to ask him to contribute materials for a brief biography. Having gained his consent, a stenographer was engaged to take down from the musician's own lips the story of his life. These notes were afterward read to Rubinstein and corrected under his supervision. We are all familiar with his activity during these latter years. Von Bulow once called him the Michael Angelo of music; and Rubinstein has said of himself: "I play as a musician, not as a virtuoso." It is this very sincerity that has won for him an exclusive position among the pianists of the world. When beneath his fingers the piano alternately sings like a human voice or thunders with all the force of an orchestra, it is not easy to realize the limited compass of the instrument. The accounts of the enthusiasm aroused by his playing seem almost fabulous. In Spain and in Italy he was cheered in the streets. His first appearance in America marks a new era in its musical history. In all the great cities of Europe the crowds that collected around the ticket offices, even when fourteen successive concerts had been announced, were so great as to require the presence of the police to preserve order. Among the delighted audiences of St. Petersburg and Moscow, who enjoyed the privilege of listening to his historical concerts, no true lover of music can have failed to appreciate that educational significance which lent to them a double value. His programmes were for the most part made up from the noted works of the great European composers; and his lectures on the history of piano-playing, illustrated as they were by his own incomparable rendering of the masterpieces of every land, won universal admiration. The Russian people can never forget its debt of gratitude to the famous composer, philanthropist, and patriot; and if illustrious men be the chief jewels in a nation's crown, then Russia may well be proud to claim as her own a man whose name will stand inscribed among the foremost in the history of Russian music of the nineteenth century.

The stimulating example of genius quickens the pulse of the nation, and Russia, the cradle of giants, still mourns the loss of Pùshkin, Lèrmontov, Skòbelev, Glìnka, Daragomìjski, Seròv, and others, all of whom died in the full tide of their vigor and activity. In 1887 Rubinstein was reappointed to the directorship of the St. Petersburg Musical Conservatory, where he still continues his valuable labors.

The supplement consists largely of what may be called the echoes of musical criticism. They are taken partly from the Russian journals, and partly from a pamphlet printed on the occasion of the Rubinstein Jubilee, an event celebrated by all classes of the vast Russian empire.

ALINE DELANO.

BOSTON, August, 1890.

CONTENTS.

CHAPTER I.

Birth. — My mother my first teacher. — My father and our family. — Removal to Moscow. — Music lessons. — V. B. Grünberg and her daughter Julia Lvòvna. — A. I. Villoing. — The first concert. — Going abroad 1

CHAPTER II.

In Paris. — Liszt, Chopin, and other celebrities. — In Holland. — Children-artists. — In London. — The musical memory. — Divided and united Germany. — In the Winter Palace. — Emperor Nicholas and the Imperial Family 12

CHAPTER III.

Return to Moscow. — My departure for Berlin. — Dehn, the teacher of counterpoint. — Mendelssohn and Meyerbeer. — My father's death. — Brother Nicholas. — My first appearance as an author. — Robert Schumann's opinion of me. — Departure for Vienna 22

CHAPTER IV.

In Vienna. — Letters of Introduction. — Hunger and authorship. — Liszt's visit. — Lessons. — Return to Berlin 29

CHAPTER V.

Residence in Berlin. — Echoes of revolution. — In the streets of Berlin. — Dehn. — Fantastical enterprises. — The flutist Heindl and Baron Fuhl . 34

CHAPTER VI.

On the frontier of the fatherland. — Arrival in St. Petersburg. — Three incidents 40

CHAPTER VII.

In St. Petersburg. — Symphony concerts in the University. — A. I. Fitztum. — K. B. Schuberth. — The Russian Opera. — The Grand Duchess Helen Pàvlovna. — Emperor Nicholas and his relations to musicians and artists. — La Blache. — Operas of "Dmìtri Donskoì" and "Thomas the Fool." — A. M. Gédéònov and the singer Bùlachov 56

CHAPTER VIII.

Life abroad. — In Moscow at the time of the coronation of the Emperor Alexander II. — At Nice in the suite of the Grand Duchess Helen. — The conception of the Russian Musical Society . . 72

CHAPTER IX.

Vassìli Aleksèyevich Kologrìvov. — Foundation in St. Petersburg of the Russian Musical Society, now the Imperial. — My first idea of founding the degree of Bachelor of Music in the department of music. — Friends and opponents of the Russian Musical Society. — Seròv. — The first concerts of the Russian Musical Society. — A new feature of musical education in Russia . . 85

CHAPTER X.

Musical classes in the Michael Palace. — The teachers and scholars. — The Music School. — The Conservatory. — The first professors and the first graduating classes of pupils of both sexes. — Relations of society to the Conservatory, and its demands upon it. — Services rendered to Russia by the Conservatory 103

CHAPTER XI.

Leaving the Conservatory. — My concerts. — Artistic tour in America. — Wieniàwski. — The different degrees of musical appreciation in the different nations 112

CHAPTER XII.

My articles on music, and my various musical works. — Historical concerts in the principal cities of Europe. — Entrance upon my second term as Director of the Conservatory. — My memoranda and projects. — Reforms in the organization of music in Russia regarded as one of the most effective instruments for popular education . . 121

SUPPLEMENT.

Rubinstein as a composer 141
Rubinstein as a pianist 163

AUTOBIOGRAPHY

OF

ANTON GRIGORIEVITCH RUBINSTEIN.

1829-1889.

———◆———

CHAPTER I.

Birth. — My mother my first teacher. — My father and our family. — Removal to Moscow. — Music lessons. — V. B. Grünberg and her daughter Julia Lvòvna. — A. I. Villoing. — The first concert. — Going abroad.

1829-1840.

I WAS born on the 16th of November, 1829, in Vichvatìjnetz, a village on the Dniester, near the frontier of the government of Podòlsk and Bessarabia. This village lies about thirty versts[1] from the city of Dubosàr, and perhaps fifty versts from Bàlta. It is only within a short time that I have learned the exact date of my

[1] One verst is about three-fourths of a mile. — TR.

birth, my ignorance of which was due to the lapse of memory on the part of my venerable mother. The result of recent examinations of the local documents seems to prove beyond a doubt that the 16th of November, 1829, must have been my birthday ; but having all my life celebrated the same on the 18th, now that I am in my sixtieth year it is rather late to alter this family fête-day, and so I shall continue to celebrate the 18th of November.

My mother Kalèria Christofòrovna, a Levenstein by birth, was a native of Prussian Silesia, where she had received a fair education, especially in music, and was thereby enabled to instruct her children; and to her I owe a debt of gratitude, — for she was my first music-teacher.

My father, Gregòri Romànovich, a Russian subject of the town of Berdìchev, had leased a tract of land in the village of Vichvatijnetz. We were a large family. Nicholas, the oldest son, died in childhood; Jacob, the second born, became a doctor, and died in 1863; I am the third, and the fourth was again called Nicholas; he was born in 1835, and has occupied the post of Director of the Moscow Conservatory. We had two sisters: Lubòv, who married the attorney Weinberg in Odessa, and Sophia, who with our mother also lives in Odessa.

The moderate income derived from the lands in Vichvatìjnetz was divided equally between my father, his brother, and his brother-in-law.

My earliest recollections are of a journey to Moscow in a roomy covered-wagon, undertaken by the three families, with all the children and servants, — nothing less than a tribal migration. We reached the city and crossed the Pokròvski bridge. Here we hired a large house belonging to a certain Madame Pozniakòv; it was surrounded by trees, and stood near a pond beyond the river Iòwza. This was in 1834 and 1835.

After our removal to Moscow, we were for a time fairly well off while the three families lived and worked together. This arrangement however did not last long. My father separated from his brother and brother-in-law, and with my mother and the children removed beyond the Ordìnka[1] into the Zamòskvorètchie,[2] where he started a pin and pencil factory.

Though our *ménage* was a modest one, we always had what for those times would have been called a fairly good piano, — square, like a table, as they were made then. When I was between five and six years old, my mother began to give me lessons in music, and not only to me, but to my brothers as well. She devoted more time to me than to the others, perhaps because she soon discerned my love for music, or at any rate the ease with which I understood and assimilated it. The lessons she gave us

[1] A part of Moscow. — TR.
[2] Literally, beyond the River Moscow. — TR.

were not only serious, but often severe, as in accordance with the method of teaching common in those days; but, as she afterwards admitted, she had never conceived any definite plan for my future musical career, — teaching me simply because she was a musician herself. Our *répertoire* included Hummel, Hertz, Moscheles, Kalkbrenner, Czerny, Diabelli, Clementi, and other musical celebrities of those days; these I studied when quite a child.

Meanwhile our good friend, Mme. Barbara Grünberg, who had married a doctor, came to Moscow with her daughter Julia, a girl of ten, even then a remarkable pianist, and who had already begun to give concerts in Moscow. She afterward married Senator Tùrin,[1] and is now a neighbor of

[1] It is at this time that Mme. Tùrin, née Grünberg, writes as follows of the great pianist and composer:

"Antoine Rubinstein était déjà élève de sa mère lorsque à Moscou nous le vîmes pour la première fois. Il était agé de huit ans, et c'était un enfant charmant, qui

mine in St. Petersburg. They often visited us, and it was Julia's progress that first inspired my mother with the idea of a more systematic musical education for me. Conscious of her own inability to continue that instruction to which, in view of my musical talent, she deemed me entitled, she made inquiries for the best piano-teacher in Moscow. The Grünbergs told her of Alexander Villoing, who at that time was thought to stand at the head of his profession in Moscow. He was invited to the house, and I think had known us before, when we lived beyond

étonnait tout le monde par la précocité de son talent. Madame Rubinstein avait tout lieu d'être fière de son fils ; mais ayant plusieurs enfants, elle ne pouvait se consacrer toute entière à l'éducation musicale du jeune Antoine. Ma mère le lui fit observer, et elle insista pour que l'enfant fût confié à Villoing, ce qui arriva en effet."

Madame Tùrin, née Grünberg, a pupil of Henselt and Mozart, became a famous pianist. She gave concerts at the courts of St. Petersburg and Vienna, and in other European cities, with great success.

the Pokròvski bridge. However that may have been, he came and heard me play. My mother then told him how she had earnestly hoped that he would consent to become my teacher, but that owing to our limited means she was unable to pay a large price for lessons. Villoing hastened to reply that he was not pressed for money, and would willingly undertake my musical education free of charge. And with him my lessons began and ended, for no other teacher did I have.

In my eighth year I began to study with Villoing, and in my thirteenth my musical education was completed, and, as I said before, I had no other teacher.

Villoing especially devoted much time and pains — with most successful results — to the correct position of my hands. He was most particular in this regard, as well as in the care he bestowed on the production of a good tone. His musical method is well known; and although he played but little himself, he was unquestionably one of the best, if not the very best professor of music. To him and to no one else am I indebted for a thorough, firm foundation in *technique*, — a foundation which could never be shaken. And let me here affirm that in all my life I have never met a better teacher. Although in his latter years he became somewhat exacting, he was at the time when I received lessons from him, the very best teacher possible. He insisted upon certain details which proved of the utmost importance to me as a student of the piano. A patient, although strict master — the latter quality no less essential than the former — Villoing was soon on such intimate terms with me that he seemed more like a friend or a second father.[1]

[1] Later, when already a man advanced in years, he married the sister of Bachmètev, the director of the Imperial Chapel Choir, — a union which resulted in misery. He died recently at the age of seventy, leaving but little money and a few violins. He died poor, as artists are wont to die. — A. R.

After we removed to the Ordinka, he visited us almost daily, and was indefatigable in his instructions. He evidently found them a pleasure and a recreation. I cannot call them lessons; they were a musical education.

On the 11th of July, 1839, I, being in my tenth year, yielded to the desire of Villoing and gave my first public concert in Moscow.[1] During the next three years I travelled with my master all over Europe. . . . Before leaving Moscow I must mention that my father was not prosperous in business; and yet I do not remember that he seemed at all anxious about his affairs. However, we children gave very little thought to our father's business matters. During the course of my studies with Villoing my mother fol-

[1] In the "Galatea," a Moscow daily of that period, we find that in this, his first public concert, Rubinstein played an *Allegro* from Hummel's Concerto, an *Andante* of Thalberg, and four minor pieces by Field, Liszt, and Henselt.

lowed them with close attention, and in his absence watched over my daily exercises and the preparation of my lessons. I have already said that in those days the method of teaching was very stern,—ferules, punches, and even slaps on the face were of frequent occurrence. . . . In these times one can form but a slight conception of the degree to which discipline, both in the home and the school, was carried. I cannot say that I personally should advocate severity, although I am a foe to lawlessness; a certain amount of discipline is needful and formerly it was enforced, but nowadays it can hardly be said to exist at all. . . .

Absorbed in my music, I do not remember when or how I learned my alphabet. While still in my eleventh year I was travelling over Europe, appearing even at that early age on the concert platform with no thought of shyness. I looked at my concerts in the light of a plaything, like a child that I was, and as I was regarded. I remember on one occasion, in 1843, when I returned to St. Petersburg with Villoing, that after a benefit concert I was, at the desire of the Empress Alexandra,[1] placed on a table and caressed by Her Majesty.

[1] Wife of Emperor Nicholas. — TR.

CHAPTER II.

In Paris. — Liszt, Chopin, and other celebrities. — In Holland. — Children-artists. — In London. — The musical memory. — Divided and united Germany. — In the Winter Palace — Emperor Nicholas and the Imperial family.

1840-1843.

MY journey abroad in December of 1840 came about in this way. My mother, anxious to make of me a first-class artist, expressed to Villoing her wish to place me in the Paris Conservatory. Villoing approving the plan offered to take me there. We left Moscow in a stage, and travelled by way of St. Petersburg. I was not however admitted into the Paris Conservatory. Whether they considered me too young, or too far advanced in music, I cannot tell, but I suspect that Villoing, who regarded me as his own creation, was reluctant to part with me, or to intrust my musical education to any other than himself, even to the teachers in the Paris Conservatory. At all events I was never admitted. . . . At that time Europe was overrun by a host of "infant prodigies," from ten to twelve years of age, gifted in various ways, who were exhibited and admired as phenomenal. . . . I was among the number. . .˙. For a whole year I remained in Paris, but had no lessons, except in music with Villoing, who jealously guarded me from all approach; not a being could gain access to me! I gave several concerts, generally in the piano rooms of some famous factory, such as Erards's and others. At one of these concerts Liszt, Chopin, Leopold Meyer, and other musical celebrities were present. This concert was given toward the end of the year 1841, before a large audience, and although many other artists besides myself sang and playèd on the occasion, the proceeds were to be used for my benefit only. . . . It was then that I played with the

Belgian violinist Vieuxtemps. . . . I cannot remember the programme. . . . One of the programmes of these child-concerts is still in existence, and I lately saw it in Holland. Villoing was highly gratified with my success; as for myself, I looked upon all this, as I have said before, in the light of an amusement. And I must confess that although my tutor was strict, I myself was a great rogue.

How many famous people I met at that time! I received many invitations and made many acquaintances, but I was too young at the time to remember very much about it. I have not however forgotten my first visit to Chopin, which has already been described in my historical lectures. . . . Nine years later Chopin died.

The year spent in Paris passed like a dream, but as far as regarded my development, it was absolutely unprofitable.

The Queen of Holland, Anna Pàvlovna,[1]

[1] A Russian grand duchess. — TR.

had not at that time lost her hearing; she understood music and was fond of it, and at her invitation I played in the palace. This, my first appearance at any court, took place at the time of the visit of her nephew, the Grand Duke Constantin, then a youth of fourteen, who accompanied by his tutor Litké was making his first tour of Europe, and whose intellect, wit, and amiability had already charmed all who saw him. The Grand Duke was most kind and attentive to me. . . .

At this time Villoing was about to take me to Germany. Liszt was then in the apogee of his glory. In the domain of music he was a king, a god; his counsels, his verdicts, were revered as the law and the gospel. It was he who advised Villoing to take me to Germany to complete my musical education. And thus we travelled through Holland, England, Norway, and Sweden into Germany, giving concerts wherever we went.

As I have before stated, infant-virtuosi were quite the fashion. Among others I recollect Sophie Bohrer, the heroine of a romantic and tragic story. Her very existence is now a matter of dispute; some assert that she is still living, others maintain that she is dead. I also remember the boy pianists, Fitch, the Englishman Palmer, the two sister violinists, Maria and Theresa Milanolo. A certain virtuosomania seems to have prevailed in 1848. Liszt stood at the head of this movement; a virtuoso playing was demanded; brilliancy and style were required. The revolution of 1848, which made great changes in the policy of nations, also gave a new direction to music; it created a demand for the very soul of art, and thus we reached the climax, the *ne plus ultra*, culminating in Wagner. . . .

In London I was graciously received by the young and then handsome Queen Victoria, and subsequently in all the aristocratic circles. Although but a boy of twelve I felt no shyness or timidity in the presence of these formal lords and ladies. My musical memory at this time and for many years later, in fact until my fiftieth year, was prodigious; but since then, I have been conscious of a growing weakness. I begin to feel an uncertainty; something like a nervous dread often takes possession of me while I am on the stage in the presence of a large audience. . . . One can hardly imagine how painful this sensation may be. I often fear lest memory betray me into forgetfulness of a passage, and that I may unconsciously change it. The public has always been accustomed to see me play without notes, for I have never used them; and I will not allow myself to rely upon my own resources or ability to supply the place of some forgotten passage, because I know that there will always be many among my audiences who, being familiar with the piece I am performing, will readily detect any alteration. This sense of uncertainty has often inflicted upon me tortures only to be compared with those of the Inquisition, while the public listening to me imagines that I am perfectly calm. Yes, this nervous agitation has developed itself since my fiftieth year. Previous to that time, more especially during the early period of which I am now speaking, these sensations were unknown. . . .

I was entirely in the hands of Villoing. He arranged the programmes for the concerts, and drilled me; I obeyed his commands without demur. But then, as I said before, I was a healthy and roguish youngster. . . .

Among the German countries we visited were Prussia, Austria, Saxony, and many other courts of the petty German sovereigns. . . . No one will refuse to acknowledge the fact that divided Germany did good service in the cause of science, literature, and art. United Germany is politically strong, but it makes no such advances in the domain of the fine arts.

In 1843, after a four years residence abroad, we returned to St. Petersburg. I was summoned to the Winter Palace and presented to the Imperial family. Emperor Nicholas received me with that inexpressibly charming affability of manner which he knew so well how to employ. He embraced me as he jestingly exclaimed, "How is your Excellency?"

At that time I was a devoted imitator of Liszt, of his manners and movements, his trick of tossing back his hair, his way of holding his hands, of all the peculiar movements of his playing, which naturally called forth a smile from those who had heard Liszt, and perhaps also increased the interest felt in the boy-virtuoso. My concerts were quite successful, and I received many gifts. Presents from the public were not in vogue at that time. I had also brought many presents from Germany, but they were inferior to those I received in Russia, particularly to those that were given me after playing in the palace. These gifts were both elegant and costly. Those which were sent later to the house, through the Court office, were less valuable.

I spoke of imitating Liszt. I had often heard him in Paris, when he was at the zenith of his glory (1839-1848), and had been deeply impressed by his playing. Rubini too made a very similar impression on me. The charm of his voice was quite beyond conception, and his power of overcoming difficulties was really marvellous. He carried his listeners by storm. Suffice it to say that when the best voices in the Italian opera were invited from Paris to St. Petersburg, Rubini's singing brought tears to the eyes of — guess whom? Emperor Nicholas himself! Fancy Emperor Nicholas shedding tears! Rubini's singing produced so powerful an effect on my senses that I strove to imitate the sound of his voice in my playing.

I remember with gratitude the many kindnesses showered upon me by the Imperial family. The Grand Duke Constantin had already spoken of me to his mother, the Empress, as well as to his brothers and sisters, and had told them of our previous acquaintance in Holland, saying many kind things in my praise, and all were most gracious to me. They were a delightful family. Both the grand dukes and their sisters were well grown and handsome. . . . The Empress was very fond of music, and the Emperor was a zealous patron and lover of art, and a fairly good musician and artist in his own person. He had a good deal of talent for music, and an excellent musical memory. I heard him once hum through the whole opera of "Fenella." He knew by heart the music of the ballet "Catherine, or the Brigand's Daughter" — but I shall return to him later.

CHAPTER III.

Return to Moscow. — My departure for Berlin. — Dehn, the teacher of counterpoint. — Mendelssohn and Meyerbeer. — My father's death. — Brother Nicholas. — My first appearance as an author. — Robert Schumann's opinion of me. — Departure for Vienna.

1843–1846.

ONCE more I found myself at home in Moscow. I had brought back no money, since the proceeds of the concerts given during our travels had been expended in travelling expenses; but I brought several valuable presents, — costly articles studded with diamonds and brilliants, such as artists in these days rarely receive. These were gifts from members of the reigning families of Russia and the other European courts, as well as from private individuals. I had received no gifts from the public. At that time laurel wreaths had not come into fashion,

— but who does not get them now! The needs of my family were urgent. The presents were pledged to a government collateral banking-house, and the money thus received was spent. It is needless to remark that the things were never redeemed.

Meanwhile my mother was not fully satisfied with my progress. My wise and anxious preceptress with unerring judgment at once perceived how very little had been done by way of perfecting my musical education, and also that if I were to go on giving concerts, I should make no further progress; and she realized the necessity for serious study. Hence she decided to go at once to Berlin, taking me, my sister Lùba, and my brother Nicholas, who besides his excellent *technique* had already given signs of ability in original composition; in fact he began to compose at the age of five.

In 1844 we settled in Berlin. This

ended our relations with Villoing, and after my thirteenth year I became my own teacher. We remained in Berlin till 1846. All this time I had lessons from Dehn, the famous teacher of harmony and counterpoint; there also, I learned the languages, which I acquired with great facility. I studied the catechism and Russian grammar with Father Dormidònt, a priest of the Orthodox Greek Church, whose daughter, Madame Kòchetov by marriage, but better known under the pseudonym of Madame Alexàndrov, became quite a prominent singer, and a professor in the Moscow Conservatory. In the other branches I had various teachers.

Many knew me in Berlin because of the concerts I had given there when a child. During this period however (1844–1846) I was giving no concerts, although I often played in society and at the clubs. The Empress Alexandra visited Berlin about this time, and my brother and myself were invited to play in her presence, and as usual were graciously received. The costly presents given us were sold at once, and were a help to us toward defraying our expenses in Berlin.

As to Dehn, my teacher in counterpoint, of whom Glìnka afterward took lessons (Dehn outlived him, dying soon after 1860), he was undoubtedly the finest teacher in harmony in Europe. Marks, another of my instructors, of whom in accordance with the advice of Mendelssohn and Meyerbeer I took lessons in the theory of music, was inferior to him.

Mendelssohn and Meyerbeer were both good friends of my mother, who often visited them in Berlin and took counsel with them concerning my musical education. Every Sunday my brother and I called upon them. Dehn was a fine scholar in his line, and had a faculty for imparting knowledge.

Dehn had other famous pupils besides

Glìnka, among whom were Friedrich Kiel and many others. He was really quite an original character. I took but few lessons from him however, for in 1846, when but a youth of sixteen, I started alone for Vienna. My individual career may be dated from that time, — a career in which joy and sorrow, abundance and penury, ay, even to hunger, followed one another; an experience by no means uncommon to men who live before the public.

My father died that same year (1846), and my mother with my sister Lùba and brother Nicholas returned to Moscow, where Nicholas entered the University. But his frequent music-lessons and numerous concert engagements left him insufficient time for the study required from a University student. However, all the professors were very kind and indulgent to him, and in some way he managed to graduate either as a *Student* or as a *Candidat*, I do not remember which.

Autobiography of Rubinstein.

At the time of my residence in Berlin my first musical composition appeared in print. It was edited by Schlesinger, one of the local musical editors, in 1843. It was a short study for the piano written in 1842 on the poetical subject of the "Undine." I suppose it must have been approved by Villoing, but it was absolutely without *Inhalt*.[1] At the same time two of

---

[1] The composition of which Rubinstein speaks thus was favorably noticed by Schumann in 1842. See Gesammelte Schriften uber Musik und Musiker von Robert Schumann (4 Band). Leipzig, Georg Wigands Verlag, 1854. — (1843.) T. IV.
 Kürzere Stücke für Pianoforte. A. Rubinstein. "Undine," — Etude für das Pianoforte. (1843.)

WERK I.

Die erste Arbeit des talentvollen Knaben, der sich als Spieler einen schon grossen Ruhm gemacht. Ob er auch bedeutendes productives Talent habe, lässt sich nach dieser vorliegenden ersten Leistung weder behaupten, noch verneinen. Doch in dem kleinen Stücke das Melodische vorwiegt, ohne gerade eine schöne neue Melodie zu bieten, lässt hoffen, dass er das wahre Wesen der Musik zu begreifen angefangen

my minor compositions were edited in Cologne, one of which was even accompanied by my portrait. It is hardly necessary to remark that neither then, nor in the course of the years immediately following, did my works bring me any return worth mentioning, and I considered myself quite lucky if I found a publisher willing to print them, an experience common to most young composers.

und sich in diesem Sinne immer glücklicher entwickeln werde. Der Titel der Etude findet seinen Grund zumeist in der wellenförmigen Art der Begleitungsfigur; etwas Originelleres, durch und durch Gelungenes konnten wir von jungen Jahren nicht erwarten. In keinem Falle dürften aber unreine Harmonien stehen bleiben, wie —

. . . .
jeder irgend leidlich gewandte Musiker hätte ihm die Stelle verbessern können.

CHAPTER IV.

In Vienna. — Letters of introduction. — Hunger and authorship. — Liszt's visit — Lessons. — Return to Berlin.

1846–1848.

I WENT to Vienna in 1846 because that city was one of the principal musical centres in Europe, and there too lived Liszt, the king of musicians, on whose help and protection I relied. These hopes however were at first dashed by the cold and distant manner with which Liszt received me. He bade me remember that a talented man must win the goal of his ambition by his own unassisted efforts. This estranged me from him. I made several other calls, having brought with me some ten or fifteen letters of introduction from N. N., the Russian Ambassador, and his wife in Berlin. I made the calls and left the letters. Then I waited for replies and invitations. Silence was the sole response. After my first, second, third, and fourth letters had met with a similar fate, I fell to pondering over the mystery. What could it mean? I was utterly at a loss. "Let me look," I thought, "and see what is said about me in these letters of introduction," quite a pile of which still remained undelivered. I opened one of them, and what did I read! The following. The ambassador and his wife introduced me with words to this effect : —

MY DEAR COUNTESS SO AND SO, — To the position which we, the ambassador and his wife, occupy, is attached the tedious duty of patronizing and recommending our various compatriots in order to satisfy their oftentimes clamorous requests. Therefore we recommend to you the bearer of this, one Rubinstein.

The riddle was solved. I understood at once the meaning of the mysterious silence, and straightway flung the remaining letters in the fire.

In Vienna I gave lessons, mostly at cheap rates; I lived in the attic of a large house, and often for two and three days in succession I had not money enough to pay for a dinner at the nearest restaurant, and so I went without. The room that I had hired was fairly bare, but soon I had crowded every corner and literally carpeted the floor with my writings. And what did I not write in these days of hunger! Every sort of composition, not only in the department of music, operas, oratorios, symphonies and songs, but articles philosophic, literary, and critical as well. In my "attic" I even wrote a paper for the benefit of a single reader, — myself. And how often I suffered from hunger! This life of poverty lasted a year and a half; and very poor I was in those days. In fact it was the old story of a friendless man struggling on without help, a story that will doubtless repeat itself as long as the world lasts. . . . It was now two months since I had called on Liszt. My prolonged absence had at last reminded him of my existence. He took it into his head to pay me a visit; and one day he made his way up to my attic accompanied by his usual retinue, his so-called courtiers, who followed him wherever he went, — a certain prince, a count, a doctor, an artist; all ardent admirers and servants of the master. The first sight of my quarters seemed to shock the whole party, more especially Liszt himself, who during his sojourn in Moscow had visited my family and knew our style of living. He showed however much tact and delicacy, and in the most friendly manner asked me to dine with him on the same day, — a most welcome invitation, since the pangs of hunger had been gnawing me for several days. After this I was always on good terms with Liszt until the time of his death. As for the music that I wrote while in Vienna, but a small part of it appeared in print. Vienna was always well supplied with publishers, but during the year between 1846 and 1847 I had only ten musical works printed, among which were several very short pieces. If I by chance received a few guldens for certain of them, I esteemed myself fortunate. A young musician just entering upon his career receives but slight remuneration for his works.

CHAPTER V.

Residence in Berlin. — Echoes of revolution. — In the streets of Berlin. — Dehn. — Fantastical enterprises. — The flutist Heindl and Baron Fuhl.

1848.

THE year 1848 found me in Berlin. I had removed from Vienna to promote my chief desire in life, — to mingle with the musical world, to give lessons, to play, and to compose.

In Berlin I found myself hurried along by the current of revolutionary ideas. Every one was agitated, and living in a state of nervous excitement. . . . I had many acquaintances among the journalists and artists, in fact among professional men in general. . . . They were all restless and feverishly excited. . . . The signal was given in Vienna and echoed back from Berlin. The revolution had burst forth. . . . I was eager to be in the streets, and what wonder? I was but nineteen. . . . I did not realize the folly of meddling with matters that were no concern of mine, or of sympathizing with aspirations foreign to my interests. My kind landlady watched over me, and would not permit her artist lodger to go out on the day when the excitement rose to the highest pitch. She simply shut me up. All that I could see from my window in the Bernstrasze was the building of the barricades. But on the following day I was out among the crowds on the square, and subsequently witnessed all the scenes of this popular revolution. . . . I saw my professor, Dehn. . . . This elderly man, a famous teacher in counterpoint, had shouldered a musket, and in his *rôle* of soldier of the National Guard, was patrolling in front of one of the government buildings.

I little realized what a grand epoch was

ushered in by the revolutionary movement of 1848, — not in politics alone, but in art as well. . . . My life may be divided into two distinct periods, and for this reason may offer hereafter a certain interest. . . .

I mentioned Dehn, who at that time in Berlin saved me from carrying out a fantastic intention which might have ended sadly for me. While I was living in Vienna, in 1847, I became acquainted with Heindl, a good flutist, with whom I made a concert tour through Hungary. Then we two, both youths at that time, and another friend, Baron Fuhl, agreed to try our fortunes in America. Our route led through Berlin, and from thence we were to go to Bremen or Hamburg, and set sail for the New World. No sooner was the idea conceived than we proceeded to carry it out. I went at once to Dehn and told him of our plans.

"See here," I said, "I am going to try my luck in America." "Heavens, are you mad!" he exclaimed. "Is it possible that you can find nothing to do in Europe? You are still but a lad, you have seen nothing of your own country, and yet you would recklessly rush off to America, where you are likely to meet with any kind of misfortune."

In short, Dehn so energetically and warmly protested against my plan that I at last recognized my folly, and parted company with my travelling companions, who were naturally quite indignant with me. Soon after this the flutist Heindl became engaged, and one day when he had started to pay a visit to his *fiancée*, while attempting to cross a drill-ground, he was accidently shot and killed by the bullet of a sharpshooter. As to the baron, he went to America, where he won for himself both social position and fortune; but, as he afterward told me, he began as a common laborer by breaking stones on the road. I saw him in 1872 during my concert tour in America; he was married, had a family of daughters, and seemed happy and contented.

Yielding to Dehn's advice I remained in Berlin, and continued to give lessons and to visit Mendelssohn and Meyerbeer. . . . Some of the lessons were well paid, but as in Berlin, and afterward in St. Petersburg, I led the bohemian life of an artist, — feasting when money was plenty, and going hungry when it was gone. I was reduced to such straits at times that I used to return the receipted tickets for lessons, accompanied by a note to the effect that my pressing engagements obliged me to discontinue my instructions for the present, and requesting to be paid before the end of the term. The money was always sent, but my patrons were often too much annoyed to employ me again.

It is hardly necessary to say that when the revolution broke out, music, as a matter of course, was wholly neglected. No lessons were sought and no concerts given; a dreary time for musicians set in. My last resource was to lose no time in returning to St. Petersburg, which I proceeded to do.

CHAPTER VI.

On the frontier of the fatherland. — Arrival in St. Petersburg. — Three incidents.

1849.

THESE events happened in 1849 or in the latter part of 1848, I am not quite sure which. I packed my scanty effects, crowded my notes, my unpublished works, — the fruits of the toil of a young composer, — into a box, and with all the artless trust of innocence set out for Russia.

I was stopped at the frontier.

"Your passport, please," demanded a fellow countryman.

"What passport?"

"What passport? You know perfectly well. Are you not aware that every person who enters Russia must have a passport?"

I had actually forgotten it; or, to speak more accurately, had never known it. When I came to Berlin with my mother, in 1844, I was a mere child. My brother, my sister, and myself were all included in the same passport with my mother. Afterward, when I went to Vienna the rest of the family returned to Moscow, and I was left without papers to prove my identity. During the three years that followed, I had had no occasion to use them in any of the cities of Germany where I had lived. But no sooner did I set my foot on native soil (I think it was in Màslovitzi) than I was confronted with the demand for a passport.

When I strove to explain, they seemed rather inclined to suspect my apparent simplicity.

"Your luggage, sir! What have you in your box? Music? It looks more like manuscripts. We will put the seals on, and it will be attended to yonder. Here is your receipt. Where are you going? St. Petersburg, by way of Warsaw? You will show them your receipt, and the luggage will be delivered to you."

I have forgotten the reason why they allowed me to pass, but I did not receive my box. I was directed to go to one Fréville in St. Petersburg, who would hand over my traps to me.

At last, after an absence of six years, I found myself once more in St. Petersburg. In 1843 I had been a petted child; I returned an unsophisticated youth, quite ignorant of the customs of my native land. And I was not long in draining the cup of experience to its bitter dregs.

I went to a hotel. I could not at first remember the name of my acquaintances. Here was I, a youth of twenty, as much alone as if I had been in the depths of a forest. Early in the morning there came a rap at the door.

"Your passport, please."

"I have none."

"What! In that case we cannot keep you any longer."

Here was a fine dilemma. I bethought myself of an acquaintance, a playmate of my childhood, Charles Lévi, an amateur musician, a little man, who died about five years ago. I started out, and found him somewhere in the Gràfski Lane.

"See here," said I to him, "they refuse to keep me at the hotel because I have no passport."

"Spend the night with me," he said, "and we will think the matter over."

In the morning came the *dvòrnik*.[1]

"Your passport."

The deuce take their passport!

"I will go to the chief of police!" I exclaimed.

General Galàhov was the chief of police at that time. I went to the bureau and informed the clerk in the reception room

[1] Janitor.

that I had recently come from abroad, and knew nothing whatever about passports or that one would be required of me. . . . He looked at me in utter astonishment.

"Wait here," he said.

When Galàhov appeared, the clerk reported to him: "A certain Rubinstein has arrived from abroad without any passport, and there he is."

"What! How is that!" roared Galàhov, "Where does he live? Where has he been? Where does he come from? Send some one to find out without delay! Inquire in whose house he has been staying! Who are they? And see that they are fined!" . . .

"What can all this mean," I thought; "why do they make such an ado over a passport? I am known to a number of men, — to Prince Lvov, Count Stròganov, Count Vielgòrski; . . . I will call upon them. What is it they require me to do?"

I never understood why Galàhov allowed

me to go. I hastened to Count Matthew Vielgòrski, and laid the matter before him. His face grew long. One must remember in what times we were living, — 1849!

"This is a serious matter," said the count, "I will write to Galàhov and tell him that I know you, and meanwhile you must write to your mother about your passport."

I wrote to my mother, and she wrote to Berdìchev asking to have individual papers sent to me. Meanwhile I returned to Galàhov, and tendered him Count Vielgòrski's letter, which he read.

"That is of no value," he said; "a letter like that is worth nothing whatever! How dare you show yourself here without a passport!" All this he shouted in stentorian tones. "Mind that you have a passport in two weeks from this time! Do you understand?"

I had no difficulty in understanding,

but I thought within myself, " Why do you get so excited ? There are officials above you." I went to Shulgìn, the governor-general. As soon as I opened my mouth he screamed, —

" I will have thee put in chains! In chains, I tell thee ! I will send thee to Siberia by *étape!*" [1]

At that time Russian generals always used " thee " to persons of my rank in life.

I was dumfounded. A youth of twenty, straight from the centre of civilization, from the world of arts and sciences, returning to his native land to find such a welcome as this!

I cannot remember how I left Shulgìn, or why he did not execute his threat. . . . That he could have done so is beyond a doubt. . . . I only remember that all this weighed on my mind. Days passed, and

[1] The Russian system of conveying prisoners to Siberia. *Étape* means a halt, a resting-place, a station. — TR.

still no passport. Meanwhile I stayed with my friends, visiting from house to house. About this time a Court ball or concert, I do not remember which, took place; and all my influential friends, to whom I had given an account of my treatment by Shulgin and Galàhov, were highly indignant.

"What are you doing with Rubinstein? He is a friend of ours; he was received at Court and played before the Imperial family. Why do you treat him in this way?" they asked.

The following day I went to Galàhov. Here I had to wait in the reception room for three hours, standing all the time, since etiquette forbade me to sit. In those days all who waited for his Excellency usually did so standing. Those were dreary times. At last I was called into his study.

"Well, my good fellow," he said, "I have been told that you are quite a musician; but I have little faith in all this talk. What I want you to do is to go to my secretary Chesnakòv and play something to him, so that we may know if you are a real musician; and bear in mind that he understands music." All this was uttered in the most scornful tones.

I was conducted to the secretary, who had some kind of miserable piano. I seated myself, and all the bitterness, the wrath, the indignation I felt at the treatment that I had received I poured forth upon the keys of that instrument. I thundered so that the piano fairly shook under my touch, and seemed on the point of falling to pieces. It was really the most wretched piano, and my wrath knew no bounds. The secretary, however, listened patiently to the end, and then we returned to the chief of police.

"Your Excellency's information was correct," he reported. "Rubinstein is a musician indeed; he can play — "

"Then let him have three weeks' grace!" thundered Galàhov.

And thus I won my reprieve. . . .

Ah, those were hard times, particularly in the year 1849! Meanwhile my passport arrived from Berdìchev, and so the demands of the law were satisfied.

This was my first adventure in my native land. The second was no less curious.

Soon after my arrival I went in quest of my treasure, the box that contained my music. As I have said before, it was in manuscript, — my work during the three years' residence in Berlin and Vienna. I do not remember who this Fréville was to whom I was sent, whether he was in the Custom House or in the Censure Department, or the secret or ordinary police. Only he did not give me my box.

"It is true my dear sir," he said, " that your manuscripts all appear to be sheet music, but it is well known to the government that the anarchists and the revolutionists write their proclamations and other papers in conventional signs that look somewhat like notes. . . . This may be some political cipher. . . . Wait patiently for five or six months, and perhaps your notes may be restored to you."

There was nothing for it but to submit. I afterward reproduced from memory such parts of my compositions as I wished to preserve, and put the ill-fated box out of my mind.

Several years later I happened one day to drop in to Bernard's music store, and there I was told that they had just bought some of my autograph compositions.

"Where did you buy them?" I asked.

"We bought them at auction, where they were sold for waste paper."

"I wish you would send and buy some for me," I said.

"I fear it is too late; it was all sold for waste paper. The paper was of a good quality."

And how did this happen? Either the Custom House or the censor, I really do not know which of the two, advertised for the owner in the "Police News;" but the owner not having the habit of reading the "Police News," the box with its contents was sold by weight at public auction. Several years later when I went to the office of the chief of police to obtain a travelling passport, one of the clerks boasted that he too had bought several of my manuscripts from a dealer in old paper. And all these came from the same ill-fated box.

Another adventure of that same unlucky year of 1849 chanced as follows.

The famous pianist Sophie Bohrer, who had given concerts in her childhood, arrived in St. Petersburg. As an old friend I was in the habit of calling upon her, and on the occasion of my first visit I met a young man there dressed in student's uniform. I will mention no name; for if he be still alive he must long since have reached the dignity of general,[1] and

[1] A remark meant to be satirical, for generals both

possibly he may be dead. He seemed anxious to make my acquaintance, and was quite attentive. He took the trouble to hunt up my quarters and showed himself very friendly. Here is a sample of his conversation : —

"You come to us here in Russia from intellectual centres, and even in our cultivated circles you will find nothing encouraging. You must feel the sudden transition from civilization and progress into a wilderness; and yet if you are so inclined, I can, even here, introduce you into society which you will find congenial and sympathetic." . . .

Suspecting no harm, I replied that I should be very glad to become acquainted with cultivated people.

"Agreed, then; on Saturday I will call and take you to my friends."

civil and military abound in Russia. It is in fact the polite mode of retiring an old and useless man. — Tr.

At the appointed hour he made his appearance. I accompanied him to the end of Great Sadòvoya Street, beyond the Church of the Pokròv. We entered an apartment in which a large number of men of all ages, both military and civilians, were assembled; I remember only one of them, a man named Palm. When I inquired for the host, who was not visible, the reply was given, "Wait awhile, and we shall all be called."

At last a bell rang, the door was flung open, and we entered a large room where a row of chairs was arranged in front of a platform, as in a concert hall. A tall, handsome man with a beard mounted the platform and read a sort of treatise advocating communistic or socialistic theories. All this surprised me greatly, and I made no attempt to conceal my feelings from my neighbors.

"I confess I never expected to find such a state of things as this in Russia," I said.

" I can understand that ideas and publications of this kind might have a *raison d'être* abroad, but surely we have no occasion for them here in Russia. They are quite impracticable and out of place in our fatherland."

I spoke thus to all who would listen to me on this evening at the house of the famous conspirator Michael Vassilievich Butashèvich-Petrashèvski, — for the tall, handsome man was no less a personage than he; and it was to these remarks of mine that I eventually owed my escape. Petrashèvski and I met, however, several times after that evening; he visited me in my apartments on the Morskàya, where he used to bring me radical books written in foreign languages, and we had many a chat and discussion on parliaments, constitutions, and kindred subjects.

Soon afterward I went to Moscow; and one day my mother said to me: " Have you heard what is going on in St. Petersburg?

A man named Petrashèvski has been arrested, and likewise many others who frequented his house. These gentlemen were members of some secret society, and are all imprisoned in the fortress."

You may imagine my feelings. I returned with fear and trembling to St. Petersburg, expecting at any moment to be arrested. On the Nevski I met my friend the student, who had introduced me to Petrashèvski; he was as cordial to me as ever, but I was now on guard. . . . Evidently my remarks had saved me, and the " Third Division," whose dreaded name carried terror to all who heard it, had spared me.

CHAPTER VII.

In St. Petersburg. — Symphony concerts in the University. — A. I. Fitztum. — K. B. Schuberth. — The Russian opera. — The Grand Duchess Helen Pàvlovna. — Emperor Nicholas and his relations to musicians and artists. — Lablache. — Operas of "Dmìtri Donskoì" and "Thomas the Fool." — A. M. Gédéònov and the singer Bùlachov.

1849–1854.

I SUPPORTED myself in St. Petersburg, as I had done in Berlin, by giving lessons. . . . Some of my pupils paid me one rouble and others twenty-five. . . . I wrote operas in German and in Italian; for at that time, with the exception of Glinka, there were no Russian composers, — nothing but amateurs, dilettanti landlords, dilettanti clerks: musicians, real artists, who looked upon their art as the very essence of their lives, were nowhere to be found. . . . The more ardent lovers of music used to congregate at the Symphony

Concerts, which were held in the University under the patronage of its famous inspector, Alexander Ivànovich Fitztum. The students formed an orchestra, and were joined by many amateurs like Doctor Behrs and myself; and so, without any rehearsals, we played on Sundays, charging a rouble for admission, and the public came flocking into the Graduation Hall of the University.

When I recall those times, I often wonder that the people should have come in such crowds to these concerts, when many of them had to cross the frozen Neva on the plank-walk. The seats were taken at once. Karl Bogdànovich Schuberth was the conductor, and when he was absent I sometimes took his place myself. And — would you believe it? — even without rehearsals, such was the love and enthusiasm that animated the performers, the orchestra really played very well. It must be remembered that previous to these University Concerts the Symphonic Assemblies had taken place but infrequently, possibly three or four times a year in the Court chapel, no oftener than that.

A very small band of amateurs, including both military and civilians, not to mention grand dukes, clustered around the Court chapel. (Grand Duke Constantin, the Emperor's son, was a very good 'cello player.) The Russian opera was as yet in embryo, as far as regards the singers, who, with the exception of Petròv, a basso of note, were beneath criticism. The famous writer, Count Sallogùb, once said of the prima donna that her voice was a draft of air, not a voice. And at this very time, when music was at so low an ebb, a new era for art was dawning within the palace of the Grand Duchess Helen, the sister of Emperor Nicholas.

A truly remarkable woman! I never in my life met her equal. To a royal dignity of manner she united the perfection of tact. She knew how to put herself in sympathy with every one who entered her presence; were he a *savant,* a soldier, an artist, a writer, a statesman, a poet, — she could converse with all, and leave a pleasing impression on every listener. Emperor Nicholas was deeply attached to her, and set a high value on her opinions. It was in her *salon* that the famous conversation took place between Emperor Nicholas and the English embassador Hamilton, concerning "the sick man," Turkey, which precipitated the Crimean war in 1853. There too the period of reform under Emperor Alexander II. was ushered in, and projects for the liberation of the serfs were discussed between the statesmen of the new reign and the cultured mistress of the *salon.* She was indeed an extraordinary woman, and exercised a great influence over the political affairs of Russia.

It must also be remarked that her *en-*

tourage was remarkable; the Baroness Ràden, one of the ladies of her court, was accounted among the cleverest women of the times, and the Grand Duchess owed much to her.

I was often invited to her *soirées* while the Grand Duke Michael was still alive. One evening he came into the *salon* with a cigar between his lips, and a big dog at his heels; he laughed and jested with the guests after his usual fashion, but soon he bade farewell to his wife and her friends, and departed for Warsaw. The next time he was seen in St. Petersburg he lay in his coffin. After his death the palace of the Grand Duchess became the centre toward which flowed the current of all the intellectual life of the capital, as at this time the Empress Alexandra was ill.

In 1852 I was engaged by the Grand Duchess as accompanist in general to the palace singers. I jestingly took upon myself the title of "Janitor of Music." Yes, I repeat, she was an extraordinarily intellectual woman; I never knew her equal. Some rank with her the Empress Augusta, an extremely intelligent lady beyond doubt, but our Grand Duchess Helen far surpassed her in intellect as well as in education. One had only to mention her name to Auerbach, or to any other European celebrity, to hear the most enthusiastic eulogies. When she lived abroad, she often invited this or that celebrity to spend a week or a month with her; writers and artists lived at her court, met and conversed with her day after day and were thoroughly charmed by her marvellous intelligence, her varied attainments, her tact and her amiability.

The musical *soirées* of the Grand Duchess were extremely interesting, for the best artists in St. Petersburg were invited to them. The majestic form of Emperor Nicholas was often seen among the guests.

He always treated me with gracious consideration, and on one occasion remained by my side at the piano for more than an hour talking, and whistling very correctly an entire opera. While his sons and daughters literally worshipped the Emperor, at the same time they stood greatly in awe of him, especially when he was out of humor.

I have a vivid recollection of two evenings in particular, when they were rehearsing tableaux at the palace of the Grand Duchess Mària Nicolàevna.[1] The Empress Alexandra, far from well, was reclining on a lounge, the young people, dukes and maids-of-honor, were laughing and rollicking in the room; it was a scene of gay merriment and confusion. I was seated at the piano playing the music set to the tableaux, then being rehearsed, when suddenly in the door-way appeared the majestic figure of the Emperor. Everything

[1] The Emperor's daughter.

Autobiography of Rubinstein. 63

came to a standstill, and a death-like silence took the place of gay confusion. The Emperor seemed care-worn and gloomy — it was the year of the Crimean war. Suddenly he turned to Roller, the decorator, and vented his wrath on him for some awkwardly arranged decoration. His mood, as may be supposed, was reflected on all present. Imagine the position of the young pianist!

As a matter of course the irate monarch paid no attention whatever to me. But when those who were to take part in the tableaux and theatricals assembled on the following day, they were nervous and ill at ease. I, dreading what might befall them, took my seat at the piano; and remembering the outbreak of displeasure on the previous evening, we awaited with trepidation the arrival of His Majesty, who, when he appeared, disappointed all expectations by his kindness and amiability. So charming was his manner to each one of us, not even excepting Roller, that he inspired us with fresh enthusiasm, and excited such genuine merriment that for many months after, this evening was remembered by many as the merriest and most animated they had known. Meanwhile, the Emperor seated himself behind me near the piano, and jested and laughed a good deal between the acts, asking me whether I remembered this or that air, and then cleverly whistling it for me.

During the winters of 1853 and 1854 these *soirées* were given alternately in the *salons* of the Grand Duchess Helen and the Grand Duchess Mària.

I remember one more episode of this same winter that serves to show what an ineffaceable impression the voice, the figure, the whole bearing of Emperor Nicholas produced on all who came into his presence.

The occasion was a *musicale* in the *salon* of the Grand Duchess Helen. The famous singer Lablache, who had been expected in St. Petersburg, had just arrived. This good-natured and finished artist was a somewhat corpulent person. Animated and quick-witted, he was a general favorite, and very much at his ease in the courts of royal personages, whether princesses, grand duchesses, or queens. The Empress Alexandra never allowed Lablache to stand in her presence; she would often place both hands on his shoulders and compel him to be seated. That evening the Emperor chanced to drop in. As he entered, Lablache rose with the rest, as a matter of course, and when the Emperor approached, and taking his hand said a few pleasant words, this clever, brilliant man,• who had felt absolutely at ease with Queen Victoria, in the presence of the Emperor, lost his self-possession entirely; his lips quivered, his voice trembled, and he could scarcely utter a word, — and this with Lablache, himself a king among men, a thoroughly independent and fearless character! But the Emperor with a courteous affability all his own, — an affability which he never failed to show to all artists and musicians, — soon restored his equanimity.

I remember an incident related to me by the architect Kusmìn, who had the habit of interlarding all his remarks with the phrase, "you understand." On one occasion when he was explaining certain architectural matters to the Emperor, he, according to custom, made free use of his favorite phrase.

"Good heavens!" exclaimed the Emperor, "of course I understand! My dear fellow, how could I help it?"

You may picture the architect's astonishment.

Another rather curious affair took place at the Grand Italian Opera House. It was the first night of Meyerbeer's "Prophet." After the fourth act the Emperor went behind the scenes, and while talking with

Mario, he asked the latter to take off his crown, which he did, and handed it to His Majesty, who, without interrupting the conversation, quietly broke off the cross, and returned the crown to the artist.

From 1852 to 1854 in St. Petersburg, I continued to lead the same old life of teaching. In spite of the fact that my pupils paid me well, I was often so much pressed for money that in the summertime I have been forced to walk from Kàmennoi-Òstrov Palace, where I lived, as the guest of the Grand Duchess Helen, into town, because I had no money to pay an *izvòschik*.[1] . . . About this time it was that one of the chief events of my life took place, — I appeared before the public as a composer. I chose for the subject of my first opera, "Dmìtri Donskoì." Count Sallogùb wrote the first and third acts of the libretto; the "Tartar scenes" in the second act were the work of Zòtov.

[1] An open hired carriage and driver. — TR.

Gédéònov was then the director of the theatre. He accepted the opera and put it on the stage.

At this time, and indeed for many years later, Russian opera was not popular; for which reason I afterward wrote my operas in Italian and in German. . . . Fiòdorov, and after him Lukashèvich, were the sole defenders of Russian opera. Indeed, one of Gédéònov's successors, Stephen Gédéònov frankly declared that it was a mystery to him that any composer should find courage to write Russian operas, since there was no possible hope of success. . . . However, "Dmìtri Donskoì, or the Battle of Kulikòvo," was written and accepted; new costumes were provided, and on April 18, 1882, the first public representation was given.

I well remember the rehearsal. I led the orchestra, and the rudeness of Gédéònov to all the artists engaged, can never be forgotten. A distinguished audience had assembled to hear it; I was already known, and my numerous friends were all present. . . . The music did not please the audience, and the singing was certainly outrageous; the only air which won an *encore* was that of the dervish, which was well sung by the young artist Bùlachov, who made his *début* on the occasion. . . . He was recalled, applauded, and made to repeat it. . . . After the curtain had fallen I hurried on to the stage to look for Bùlachov, that I might thank him. I found the young man hidden in some corner behind the scenery. . . . He was agitated, trembling, and in tears. . . .

"What is the matter?"

"Director Gédéònov has just been abusing me in such terms as no *izvòschik* would use!"

"What reason did he give?"

"It was because I took my hat when I bowed to the audience. 'A dervish,' he said, 'should never bow;' and I might have ruined that new hat; he was amazed at my boldness. And this is the way things go on; how can any one be expected to work under such conditions?"

But the saddest part of all was the result of these reproaches on the spirits of this young artist, whose *début* had given promise of a successful career. The abuse of the director discouraged him to such a degree that he took to drink, and has never risen above the rank of a second-rate artist.

Eventually, however, the opera of " Dmìtri Donskoì " proved fairly successful. Soon after this the Grand Duchess Helen invited me to act as accompanist to the singers at her musical *soirées*, and also asked me to write a series of short operas to illustrate the various nationalities of our great country. I wrote three one-act operas; the first, descriptive of Caucasia, " Hadjì Abrèk," in which I used Lèrmontov's poem for my theme; the second, of Siberia, called "Siberian Huntsmen," founded on a libretto of André Gérébzòv, and the third, "Thomas the Fool," the libretto of which was written by the well-known poet Michàilov, who was banished in 1861 to Siberia, where he soon afterward died.

The *motif* for the latter opera was taken from Little Russian life. It was first given in 1853, but the singing was so outrageously bad that I actually ran away from the theatre, and appeared the following day at the office and persistently demanded the return of the score. . . . I was afterward informed that the public received the opera kindly. Semiònov, who at that time occupied the position of subordinate clerk, tried in vain to pacify and reason with me. . . . He seemed to be the only man in the office at that time who took the slightest interest in Russian opera; but I was not to be appeased.

CHAPTER VIII.

Life abroad. — In Moscow at the time of the coronation of the Emperor Alexander II. — At Nice in the suite of the Grand Duchess Helen. — The conception of the Russian Musical Society.

1854–1858.

THE intervening years, from 1854 to 1858, I spent abroad, making a musical tour through Germany, France, and England, visiting all the principal centres of these countries. Directly after this journey I was summoned to Moscow by the Grand Duchess Helen, to be present at the coronation of the Emperor Alexander II., but arrived only in time for the festivities of the second day.

During my sojourn abroad in 1854, I spent five or six months in Weimar. Let me here remark, that at the time of the Crimean war all Europe was hostile to Russia, or rather to her foreign and domestic policy. Everything Russian was regarded with an unfriendly eye, in Prussia no less than in other countries. A few of the officers and generals decorated with Russian orders were the only persons who showed any degree of sympathy for our fatherland; all the others were decidedly hostile. However, this hostility did not extend to the domain of music, although, oddly enough, I was considered a Russian in Germany and a German in Russia.

Weimar was the paradise of art, literature, and music. Here was the home of Liszt, wherein he reigned supreme. No shrine was ever more devoutly visited; authors, painters, musicians, — all came hither as guests of the Duke of Weimar.[1] The Duke himself, a man of cold and formal bearing, playing as he did the part of a potentate in this microscopic kingdom, could not fail to appear rather ridiculous, although he was sincerely fond of art

[1] Brother of the late Empress Augusta of Germany. — TR.

and literature, and especially devoted to music. During the residence of Goethe in Weimar it was facetiously said of the reigning duke, "We, by the grace of Goethe, Duke So and So." The present duke seemed eager to formulate something of the same nature in regard to Liszt, who was worshipped as a demi-god.

The Princess Witgenstein, a Polish lady, whose maiden name was Ivanòvska, wife of an *aide-de-camp* of the Russian Emperor, and mother of the present Princess of Hohenloe, lived in Weimar at that time. She was a woman of such ability and education that to venture upon a conversation with her was a serious matter. She was something more than a blue-stocking. She was not handsome, but her influence over Liszt was unbounded. She it was who persuaded him to abandon a certain dilettanteism in music, and goaded his genius toward the more serious vocation of a composer; hence they may both be looked upon as sponsors in some sort to Wagner and the music of the future, of which Weimar was the cradle. (Madame Olivié and Madame Wagner were both daughters of Liszt.) I spent five or six months there, living with Liszt, and dining at the house of Madame Witgenstein. The personality of Liszt, it must be granted, was most unusual. His career as a *virtuoso* had ended some forty years prior to this time, and now, septuagenarian as he was, he had taken it up again. At this time, however, the impression he produced was due rather to his clerical title, his long silvery hair, and his advanced age. . . . I think it was in 1871 that Liszt was invited to visit Vienna; I was there, and conducted the orchestra at one of the concerts given in honor of his visit. We met as old friends sincerely attached to each other. I knew his faults (a certain pomposity of manner for one thing), but always esteemed him as a great performer, —

a performer-virtuoso, indeed, but no composer. I shall doubtless be devoured piecemeal for giving such an opinion. . . .

My object in removing to Western Europe at that time was to introduce myself as a composer. Germany, with its numerous petty sovereignties, was then a kind of Eldorado for the arts and sciences. . . . Each court vied with the other in protecting science and the fine arts. . . . Each university strove to attract to itself the shining lights of science. The universal standard of intelligence and intellectual development in general was carried to a much higher pitch in divided Germany than in these later times, now that it is compressed as by an iron ring into a single great kingdom. . . . Howsoever absurd may have been the political aspirations of divided Germany, in the domain of intellectual development she knew no superior. Petty sovereignties as a rule progress more rapidly than those of greater extent. What was Italy before her unification, and what is she now? It was this very intellectual greatness, however, that laid the foundation for the political strength of Germany and her present unity, which already weighs so heavily on intellectual progress.

While abroad from 1854 to 1855 I not only visited Germany, but London and Paris as well, giving concerts wherever I went. During the time of my stay in Vienna I wrote for one of the musical journals an article on the condition of music in Russia, in which I spoke of Glìnka with reverence, praising him to the skies, and comparing him to Beethoven and other masters; but the other composers fared ill at my hands. I was justly severe upon the ignorant dilettanteism of clerks and landlords, who, saving Glìnka, the great creator of Russian opera, were the chief rulers in the musical circles of Russia. Not having the habit of repentance for the occasional follies of which I am guilty, I cannot say that I regret the article, although I must fain admit that it was a great piece of indiscretion on my part. . . . Well, I was severely criticised for this article in my own country. Torrents of vituperation descended upon my head; all those Russian dilettanti composers and amateurs whose claims I had ignored, with the exception of Glinka, were so enraged that they were about to bring a suit against me. I do not remember who interfered to avert the catastrophe, but I think it was the Grand Duchess Helen. . . . To my utter surprise, however, Glinka himself was angry with me.

I had known Glinka in St. Petersburg, and had always had the highest regard for him, and he, too, had been very friendly with me; but when I called on him in Berlin, I found him ill and irritable. He received me coldly, and actually reproached me for the very article in which I had spoken so enthusiastically of his genius and compositions. Thus we parted; I, deeply grieved, and saying, as I bade him good-by, that I was wholly unprepared to learn that I had incurred his displeasure, for I had, and always should have, the highest admiration for his genius.

In after years I proved my sympathy for the author of the " Life for the Czar " by something more substantial than words. I was the first person to start a subscription fund for his monument, five thousand roubles (the proceeds of a concert I gave) forming the nucleus. I may say without vain-glory that had it not been for my efforts, Heaven alone knows when the monument would have been raised. And yet on the day when it was unveiled, I received from the managers no other invitation than the ordinary notice. During August and September of 1856, I spent three weeks in Moscow. Among the other festivities by which the coronation of the Emperor Alexander II. was celebrated, were several concerts at the palace of the Grand Duchess

Helen. Emperor Alexander II. was not particularly fond of music. At the concerts given by the Grand Duchesses Mària or Helen, he would generally play his usual game of whist in the adjoining room, and when he passed through the concert hall after the last rubber, it was a signal for the concert to close. Sometimes he would say a word or two of praise to one performer or another. It must be borne in mind, however, that he was preoccupied with questions of the greatest importance to the general welfare of our country, and had but little time to devote to music; and yet his reign marks an era even in this art, for one of the chief objects of his *régime* was to excite the spirit of activity in Russian society, to animate it with a new life, and to set it free not only from the bonds of serfdom, but also from many another fetter which had till then constrained it. Thus his reign forms a brilliant epoch in the annals of Russian music. After the

Autobiography of Rubinstein. 81

coronation, the Empress-Dowager Alexandra and the Grand Duchess Helen proceeded to Nice. I too received an invitation from the Grand Duchess to spend some time at her court, in which I held the office of "Janitor of Music," a title I had jestingly given myself.

I have charming recollections of this winter from 1856 to 1857, which was spent in Nice. The Empress Alexandra, bowed down with grief for the death of her husband and the result of the Crimean war, still liked to keep the young people around her bright and cheerful; and many of the members of the Imperial family visited her there. Among others the Grand Duke Constantin came, and the Grand Dukes Nicholas and Michael spent weeks at a time, accompanied by their suites. I well remember some of them, — Count Matthew Vielgòrski, Adjutant Apràksin, and others. There was no end to jokes and merriment. . . . Once we arranged a mock serenade to amuse the Empress. We all wore masks, and each one played on the musical instrument with which he was least familiar. Thus Vielgòrski took a bass-viol, I a kettle-drum, the Grand Dukes each one odd instrument or another, and the masked orchestra entered the apartments of the Empress. She was somewhat startled at the first sounds of this chaotic music, but afterward laughed and joked over the wild prank. . . . The Empress Alexandra was always affable and charming in her manners. . . . While staying at Nice the Court spared no money. King Victor Emmanuel came there repeatedly, and did all in his power to amuse his Imperial guests; although during the Crimean war he had been the ally of our enemies, now that the war was over he strove by every means to efface all unfavorable impressions from the heart of the widow of the Emperor Nicholas. . . . It was then that I made the acquaintance of

Cavour, the creator of Italian unity. . . .
On the whole, our season in Nice was extremely pleasant. We had constant visitors from Russia; the Grand Duchess Helen even bought a villa there. . . . We played, sang, and enjoyed music to our hearts' content; and long and frequent were the discussions about the music of our fatherland. The Grand Duchess Helen, with her usual sympathy, became deeply absorbed in this matter. Count Matthew Vielgòrski and I, as well as others who belonged to her circle, took an active part in these conversations. We talked a great deal about it, and all acknowledged that the state of music in Russia was deplorable. We all unanimously agreed — the Grand Duchess particularly favoring it — that on our return to St. Petersburg something must be done for the musical education of Russian society; and it was there in Nice, under the beautiful skies of Italy, that the first conception of the Russian

Musical Society in St. Petersburg took its origin. . . . In 1857 the Grand Duchess returned to St. Petersburg; and I, after having visited Paris and London, also returned to Russia.

CHAPTER IX.

Vassìli Aleksèyevich Kologrìvov. — Foundation in St. Petersburg of the Russian Musical Society, now the Imperial. — My first idea of founding the degree of Bachelor of Music in the department of music. — Friends and opponents of the Russian Musical Society. — Seròv. — The first concerts of the Russian Musical Society. — A new feature of musical education in Russia.

1858–1859.

ONE of the first to comprehend and sympathize with our project for founding the Russian Musical Society was Kologrıvov, an energetic worker, whom I had known well since 1852. A land proprietor in the government of Tùla, for some time a clerk in one of the civil departments, but now retired, Vassìli Aleksèyevich was an excellent 'cellist and an ardent lover of music. . . . At first he made an attempt to animate the Russian opera troupe. He had in some way connected himself with the theatre;. but on one occasion, in the presence of all the troupe, Fiòdorov spoke to him so sharply that Kologrìvov gave up both the theatre and his project. The noble individuality of Kologrìvov was never recognized by our public or by the press, and now he seems to be almost wholly forgotten. I may add that even during his lifetime Kologrìvov was but little appreciated. . . . Full of indomitable energy, and with an ardent fanaticism verging upon rudeness, he devoted himself to the pioneer task of establishing and organizing the Musical Society. He drafted into the society every man he could find; he fairly took possession of people in the streets; he would explain, demonstrate, almost drag them in by main force; he was a man of expedients. In a word, he labored for the society, not only previous to its foundation, but during the early years of its existence. He worked in the true spirit of self-sacrifice, and regardless of his own interests, devoted his entire fortune to the cause. He died a poor man. His widow, a worthy lady, is working at this very day as a music-teacher in the Kiev Institute. . . . We owe a debt of gratitude to the memory of Kologrìvov; in the first place for his labors in founding the Musical Society, and secondly for the establishment of the conservatories in St. Petersburg, Moscow, and Kiev. Incredible as it may seem, the enemies of the new society were to be found on every hand. They spoke, declaimed, wrote, and printed against it; they even condemned our audacity in calling the new society "Russian." And had it not been for the enlightened patronage of the Grand Duchess Helen and the energy of Kologrìvov, the enterprise could never have been carried out so rapidly and successfully as it was.

It must be admitted that we conducted our affair with great circumspection. We were well aware of the tedious delays awaiting us in the various departments if we should ask for the ratification of new by-laws for the society, — for the atmosphere was still charged with the traditions of the Nicholas *régime,* when the foundation of any society whatsoever was a matter of extreme difficulty. We called to mind the existence of a certain Society of Musical Amateurs connected with the Court chapel, who were favored by the government, and were in the habit of giving symphony concerts. In the beginning they had a fine orchestra, conducted by old Louis Maurer; but for the past few years this society had been practically dead, and our plan was to restore it to life, that we might take advantage of its ready-made by-laws. All we asked was permission to continue what had been previously allowed, — that is to say, to come together for the purpose of playing and singing.

" Certainly, if you wish to sing and play

you may do so; you have already had permission to do that," was the answer we received. And thus it was to all appearance on the old foundations, and under the guise of the old set of musical amateurs, who had, so to speak, come to life again, that we started the new Russian Musical Society, which now bears the title of " Imperial." Within the Michael Palace those classes were formed which may be regarded as the nucleus of the St. Petersburg Conservatory, founded in 1862.

In the same palace a mixed choir of amateurs was quickly formed, and lectures delivered before the classes. Leschetizki was professor of the piano, Madame Nissen-Sàlomon of vocal music, Wieniàwski of the violin, etc; I assumed the directorship of this embryo conservatory. In order to raise funds for the establishment, we used to give concerts nearly every day; and the excitement and competition were widespread and universal.

But the birth of this new musical association was an extremely critical event. Music was at a low ebb in Russia. The professional artist was unknown; we had amateurs in plenty, not to mention Mæcenas-musicians, also a crowd of devotees to the Italian opera, — landlords and *chinòvniks-melomans*, — but as to professional musicians, there was not one to be found. Kologrìvov and I, pioneers and innovators as we were, devoted our energies to starting an institution in which a musician might win the degree of Bachelor of Music, — a title similar to that bestowed by the Academy of Fine Arts on painters, sculptors, and architects.

I will relate in passing the seemingly insignificant incident that first gave me the idea of defining the status of a musician in Russian society, so that by itself alone, without the addition of merchant, clerk, or landowner, this title would ensure for its bearer a recognized position.

On one occasion while I was performing my religious duties, I went to the confession in the Kazàn Cathedral. After confession I proceeded to the table to have my name enrolled in the books.[1] The deacon began his inquiries.

"Your name, rank, (*chin*) and vocation?"

"Rubinstein, artist," I said.

"Are you employed in the theatre?"

"No."

"Then perhaps you give lessons in some school?"

"I do not," I replied.

The deacon appeared surprised, but no more so than I. We both remained silent.

"I am a musician, an artist," I repeated.

"Yes, I understand; but are you in the government service?"

---

[1] The Russian law obliges every adult belonging to the Greek Church to go to confessional once in three years. The records of names are set down in books kept for that purpose. — TR.

"I told you that I was not."

"Who are you then? How shall we describe you?"

For several minutes the questioning went on. I know not how it would have ended had it not occurred to the deacon to say, —

"May I ask your father's profession?"

"A merchant of the second guild."

"Now, then, we understand!" exclaimed the deacon, greatly relieved. "You are the son of a merchant of the second guild, and as such we shall inscribe your name."

These questions and the careful definition of my social position left an indelible impression upon my mind. Evidently the name and estate of a musician, universally acknowledged in other lands, had in Russia no clearly defined meaning. Who was Glìnka after all? A landowner, a nobleman in the government of Smolènsk. Seròv? An official in the Post-office Department. . . . In fact, all who had to do with music, whether as performers or composers, were either noblemen, government officials, *attachés* of the theatre, or pedagogues in public or private schools, etc. Was it possible that a man who had adopted music for his profession had no recognized position in Russia as a musician pure and simple.

The deacon of the Kazàn Cathedral called forth this thought in me, put this problem before me, and several years later Kologrìvov and myself solved it. The conservatory in Russia created from its pupils a new class of citizens called " Bachelors of Music." It was not until 1860 that the Russian musician won for himself that acknowledged position which the painter had held for a hundred years, and which, thanks to the influence of Sumaròkov, the founder of the Russian theatre, had also been enjoyed by the Russian actors.

Kologrìvov was indeed a man of remarkable character, energetic, inspired with the enthusiasm of the pioneer, and loving music with his whole soul. . . .

Men who are ready to strike out for themselves in unbeaten paths and to devote all their energies to the attainment of their goal are by no means common in Russian society; in truth, I know none such. . . . A fine musician and finely educated man, intimate with the best musical circles of Europe, Kologrìvov had encouraged and protected both Pikkel and Weikman, those famous pillars of the orchestra, now aged men. Karl Schuberth, the never-to-be-forgotten Fitztum (Inspector of University students), Lavonius, Skordùli (whose daughter was a known singer in her day), Shùstov, the architect's son, all belonged to Kologrìvov's set. . . . This circle was made up of men who inhaled music with every breath they drew, for whom it was the very alpha and omega of their existence. . . . Such men have, I grieve to say, utterly died out!

It cannot be denied that the present time (I am speaking of the musical world) is in many respects far in advance of the old days of 1859 and 1860; art is more widely diffused, and its devotees are more numerous, — but alas for the ardent love that once filled our hearts! Very little trace of that remains. . . .

I have already spoken of the enthusiasm kindled in the hearts of those who, under the patronage of the Grand Duchess Helen, had labored in behalf of the Russian Musical Society and its early classes in her palace. . . . The best musical talent in St. Petersburg was offered almost free of charge for the promotion of the good work; Zarèmba, Leschetìzki, Nissen-Sàlomon, Wieniàwski, and others asked but a rouble a lesson in the classes at the Michael Palace. And these classes were soon crowded with pupils of different ages and degrees of social standing, all eager to gain a higher musical education. . . . An orchestra and choruses were organized. . . . The Grand Duchess took a deep interest in this enterprise; she frequented the classes, contributed to their support, and bestowed her patronage not only by smiles and gracious demeanor, but by substantial pecuniary aid. . . . Ah, the definition of patronage has suffered a change since those days; it no longer signifies money, and more's the pity, since money is the nerve of every enterprise.

At the head of this musical society stood Count Matthew Vielgòrski, Kologrìvov, Stàsov, Kànshin, and myself. Kànshin had intended to start a separate society in St. Petersburg; but in order to promote unity of action as well as to avoid weakening our forces by division, we invited him to join ours. When he joined us, he promised to influence a large number of men of fortune; and although the event proved him unable to fulfil his promise, he was individually a very useful member. . . .

We leaders, together with our co workers, visited several of the wealthy residents of St. Petersburg, soliciting contributions; and the first year we collected quite a respectable sum, — several thousand roubles. We were like priests going from house to house glorifying Christ [1] and collecting alms; we visited Prince Yusùpov, Bernadàki, Gròmov, and others. Some gave one hundred, some three hundred, and some five hundred roubles. Several ladies in the higher circles labored indefatigably in behalf of our conservatory. Madame Vérigin (wife of a member of the Council of State) collected by subscription about three thousand roubles at one time; Madame Abazà, *née* Stubé, undertook the charge of our modest treasury; Princess Elizabeth Witgenstein, *née* Eyler, collected rouble after rouble for our

[1] At Christmas and Easter, Russian priests go from house to house, singing certain short prayers, for which they receive a small sum. This is called "glorifying Christ." — TR.

enterprise. The enthusiasm and energy were truly remarkable, and yet we found no lack of opponents. . . . Opposition sprang up in various official circles; for instance, it was reported that the Director of the Court chapel, Lvov, had threatened to discharge any of his singers who dared to take part in our concerts during Lent. A "free school" started up as rival: "You demand payment for instruction, but we invite pupils to come to us, free of charge!" With scant courtesy Seròv thundered against us everywhere, in the public ways as well as in print. "They are a set of Germans, professional pedants!" he declaimed on every side; and all this because we had not invited him to become a director in the Musical Society, or offered him any position whatsoever. . . . Theophilus Tolstoi, who wrote musical criticisms under the name of Rostislàv, was another of our detractors; the fact was that every man was eager to gain a place, and we had none to give. When we afterward learned the secret of their animosity, we began to create places for our opponents. We appointed several committees connected with the society; one, for instance, to examine musical compositions, another to draw up programmes, etc. We invited the railers to become members of these committees, and thus succeeded in pacifying their outbursts of envy by gratifying their personal ambitions.

A word about Seròv. He was undeniably a talented man; he had a thorough knowledge of the stage, and of everything appertaining to it. Possessed of a certain kind of instinct, he might have gone very far in the composition of operas; but unfortunately, the want of æsthetic training was only too evident; his productions lack refinement, and give but slight evidence of artistic feeling. . . . I do not know what ideals of art he may have cherished in youth, but he was consumed by a morbid self-esteem and ambition. . . . Carried away by his desire to be conspicuous, what surprising statements has he not made in his essays on music and in his lectures on art! He even went so far as to protest against music schools. . . . Out of the great mass of his writings I have read but very little, and even this little seemed absurd to me. . . . This remarkable man was an extremist. At times he hardly seemed to realize the full significance of what he was doing and saying; as for instance when he denied the advantage of conservatories, and of musical education in general.

In the first three years of the existence of the Russian Musical Society, the concerts were given in the house of Yellissèyev, near the Police Bridge, where the Club of the Nobles is now located. The audiences were large, filling the hall to its utmost capacity. One original feature of these very successful concerts was the programme containing bibliographical details concerning the composers whose works were given. But however great the success of these concerts, it was but as a drop in the ocean compared with the influence that, thanks to the activity of the Russian Musical Society, gradually effected a transformation in the method of teaching music throughout all Russia, in the institutes,[1] schools, and in families. . . . Hitherto, the musical training of the girls and boys had amounted to no more than the drumming of some foolish air to celebrate papa's or mamma's birthday, or to do honor to the principal of the school; but in these days a musical education is a more serious matter. We all know that it is regarded as an important factor in every school and institute. The former pupils of the St. Petersburg Conservatory, and other numerous establishments throughout Russia, of which that is the prototype, have effected a complete change in the methods of musical instruc-

---

[1] High schools exclusively for daughters of the nobility. — Tr.

tion in Russia. . . . Great changes have taken place in Moscow under the direction of my deceased brother, Nicholas Rubinstein, and his able successors. He acted in accordance with my advice: "Make haste and enlist as many members as possible," I said. "Summon all your energy and courage, and lose no time in organizing your musical society." His success was partly due to the fact that there was no competition in Moscow, and largely to the generous response of the citizens to his appeal in behalf of musical education.

CHAPTER X.

Musical classes in the Michael Palace. — The teachers and scholars. — The Music School. — The Conservatory. — The first professors and the first graduating classes of pupils of both sexes. — Relations of society to the Conservatory, and its demands upon it. — Services rendered to Russia by the Conservatory.

1859–1867.

MEANWHILE the "musical classes" of the Michael Palace were gradually developing into a conservatory. . . . By-laws were drawn up, and an establishment founded. It must be remembered that this was a time of ultra-patriotism. . . . In framing the by-laws we deemed it wiser to avoid foreign words, and consequently would not think of calling our school a "Conservatory," and therefore we called it the "Music School." Neither would our teachers bear the title of "professor," since that too is a foreign word, but must be called "instructors." The by-laws were presented and ratified in 1862, and the result proved that in our struggle to adhere to the vernacular, we had, to some extent, injured our position; for the title of professor in Russia indicates a far more honorable rank than that of instructor. However, in 1873, after the death of the Grand Duchess Helen, when the Grand Duke Constantin became the patron of the Conservatory, the by-laws were amended. The Music School was turned into a Conservatory, and the "instructors" into "professors."

I was its first director, serving from Sept. 1, 1862 to 1867. Gerke, Leschetizki, Dreischok, Davydov, Nissen-Sàlomon, Wieniàwski, Schuberth, Peterson, Weikman, Zabel, Chiardi, Zarèmba, Villoing, Luft, Metzdorf, Voyàchek, Cavalini, Fererro, Repetto, Van-Ark, Kross, Zeifert, Fàmintsin, Rubètz, Johanson, Czerny, and other musicians well known in Russia, were by turns professors and tutors of the first Russian conservatory.

The members of our first class were really artists and connoisseurs : Tchaikòvski, Rybàsov, Laroche, Madame Lavròvski, Madame Èssipov, Mademoiselle Tèrminski, Mademoiselle Malozyëmov (now one of its teachers), Mademoiselle Ìritzki, Mademoiselle Minkvitz, Mademoiselle Timànov (she too was afterward professor, and has since removed to Berlin), Albrecht, Mademoiselle Spàsski (a fine musician, who founded a music school in Vilno), Puchìlov, Sàlin (violinists), Hommelius (organist), Makàrov, Kross (he and Tchaikòvski received medals), may be mentioned among others. This affluence of talent in the first class may be ascribed to the fact that in the beginning of 1860 Russian society sent from its midst as pupils to the Conservatory, men and women of ripe talents; it had waited long for just such an institution, and rapid indeed was its growth.

Toward the end of the first term of my directorship, the number of pupils increased to two hundred; and it continued to increase until seven hundred pupils of both sexes had enrolled their names. This seems to me to have been a serious mistake. A conservatory should grow in height, so to speak; and instead of this it grew in breadth, and became a music-factory. And now, when after many years I am again its director, I shall certainly bring all my influence to bear to restore the factory to a studio, and I am not without hope of success.

Returning to the period of the foundation of the Conservatory in St. Petersburg, I will relate a few incidents in order to illustrate the relations of Russian society to this new institution. Many of our ladies openly expressed their surprise that an establishment for musical education should be thoroughly Russian. On introducing her young daughter to me, some fashionable lady would remark in French, —

"Monsieur Rubinstein, I have brought my daughter; I hope she will benefit by your musical instruction, and also keep in practice with languages."

"But all our lessons are given in Russian."

"What, music in Russian!" exclaims the astonished lady. "That is an original idea!"

And surely it was surprising that the theory of music was to be taught for the first time in the Russian language in our Conservatory. Professor Zarèmba, a Protestant, and something of a fanatic, taught it in Russian. Hitherto, if any one wished to study it, he was obliged to take lessons from a foreigner, or to go to Germany. . . . Zarèmba understood his business thoroughly, and his services were invaluable to the Conservatory.

It was by no means unusual to learn that our new establishment was regarded as a place especially adapted for weak-minded children. "Monsieur Rubinstein," some afflicted mamma would say, as she brought in her half-witted boy, "I was obliged to take my son away from such and such an establishment on account of ill health" (in others words for incapacity); "what shall I do with him? I had thought that if I were to place him in your Conservatory, it might be easier for him. He could take up a few branches, and might possibly develop a talent for music."

Under these circumstances what could be done? Of course I must say to these ladies that only an intelligent and studious child, sound in body as well as in mind, can be admitted to the Conservatory.

Our decision to introduce other branches of instruction besides music proved very attractive to parents of an economical turn of mind, who argued that it must cost less to send their children to the Conservatory than to other schools. Certain privileges relating to military service had been granted to the Academy of Fine Arts, and when the same privileges were bestowed on us, young men were to be found, who, without one spark of musical talent, knowing that a diploma would secure to them exemption from two years military duty, sought refuge beneath the hospitable roof of the Conservatory. Of course such cases were not numerous; . . . still they did occur, and surely the cause of music gained nothing from them! The Conservatory expanded, especially during my absence; and the rapid increase of students had its essential disadvantages. Under the directorship of Zarèmba, Azanchèvski and Davỳdov, no doubt much good was accomplished, and yet many mistakes were made. One serious mistake was the comparative ease with which diplomas were won, since many of the students (I am speaking of the men), were not animated with the love of art, or possessed of a talent for it. They valued their diploma solely as a means of shortening their term of military service. Such students as these, as I said before, were of no advantage to the cause of music. Another mistake was the introduction of scientific branches into the curriculum of the Conservatory. A conservatory should be a musical university in the strict sense of the word; a young person should not be admitted without a certain degree of education, and there should be no opportunity for preparatory classes.

After all, our conservatories have done good service. Through their influence the light of musical education has spread throughout all Russia. The St. Peterburg Conservatory alone, — not to mention that of Moscow, and the schools at Kiev, Khàrkov, Saràtov, Tiflìs, Odessa, and even in Omsk (Siberia), — has given birth to a group of remarkable musicians, a few of whom I will mention: Tchaikòvski, a graduate of the *École des Droits*, a composer of genius, known throughout Europe, although barely fifty years of age; Madame Lavròvski the contralto; Madame Èssipov the pianist; the late Hubert, director, and successor of Nicholas Rubinstein at the Moscow Conservatory; Kross the pianist, and former professor in the St. Petersburg Conservatory; Laroche, a highly educated man, who wields a clever pen as musical critic, and understands the theory of music better than most professors (he had been professor in the Moscow Conservatory); Altani, a remarkable orchestra leader, and many others. The competent teachers who have been graduated from the Conservatory may be reckoned by the dozens; . . . but in regard to singing, it is difficult to say who are the superior and who the inferior teachers. They may be compared to physicians, — not even the most successful among them can ensure life; and the best master in the world may ruin the voice of his pupil when trying to cultivate it.

CHAPTER XI.

Leaving the Conservatory. — My concerts. — Artistic tour in America. — Wieniàwski. — The different degrees of musical appreciation in the different nations.

1867–1872.

IN the month of September, 1867, having disagreed with some of its professors as to the objects and methods of instruction, I left the Conservatory. This breach was partly caused, no doubt, by my hasty temper; for I am ever in deadly earnest, and the affairs of the Conservatory lie very close to my heart.

While I was connected with the Conservatory, and ever since that time, I have had the habit of giving many concerts. I have given them in all the principal countries of Europe, with the exception of Greece, Roumania, and Turkey. I have also given a great many charity concerts. And here let me call attention to one of the distinguishing features of Russian society; that is, the frequency with which one is called upon to give concerts in aid of the students of the various educational establishments. This is a charity to which I have never been asked to contribute outside of Russia. Whenever I have given concerts abroad for benevolent purposes, it has usually been for the benefit of the poor of one town or another, or to aid the sufferers from some calamity, or for the benefit of an artists' fund, etc.; but neither in Germany, nor in any other country save Russia, have I been asked to play for the benefit of students.[1] This is all the more

[1] It has been ascertained that during the twenty-eight years which have elapsed since the foundation of the Conservatory, Rubinstein devoted the proceeds of his charity concerts, amounting to more than three hundred thousand roubles, to the benefit of the poor, and to other good works. His brother Nicholas also gave generously to the cause of charity. During the winter of 1877–78 his Saturday and Sunday concerts in Moscow netted the sum of fifty-two thousand roubles for the benefit of the Red Cross Society.

surprising, because university education abroad is very expensive. . . . I cannot explain the matter; I only know that at home I have repeatedly been asked to assist at such concerts, and have often given them myself. . . .

In 1872 the late violinist Henri Wieniàwski [1] and I accepted a manager's proposal to make a concert tour in the United States. Only two Russian artists had ever visited America, — Prince Galitzin and Slaviànski-Agrènev. The contract with the American manager was concluded in Vienna through the agency of the attorney Jacques. I was to receive two hundred thousand francs, half of which sum was deposited by the manager in the bank then and there. According to the terms of the contract, he had no right

[1] Wieniàwski was then undoubtedly the finest violinist. His playing was extremely brilliant; he was a bright, witty man, but somewhat feeble. While in America he was quite well, and received for his tour one hundred thousand francs. He died of dropsy in Moscow.

to take me to the Southern States, the whole route being clearly defined by this legal document. For a time I was under the entire control of the manager. May Heaven preserve us from such slavery! Under these conditions there is no chance for art, — one grows into an automaton simply, performing mechanical work; no dignity remains to the artist, he is lost. . . .

During the time I remained in America we travelled through the United States as far as New Orleans, and I appeared before an audience two hundred and fifteen times. It often happened that we gave two or three concerts in as many different cities in the same day. The receipts and the success were invariably gratifying, but it was all so tedious that I began to despise myself and my art. So profound was my dissatisfaction, that when several years later I was asked to repeat my American tour, with half a million guaranteed to me, I refused point blank. It may be interesting to note that the contract was fulfilled to the letter.

Wieniàwski, a man of extremely nervous temperament, who, owing to ill health quite often failed to meet his appointments in St. Petersburg, — both at the Grand Theatre and at the Conservatory, — never missed one concert in America. However ill he might be, he always contrived to find strength enough to appear on the platform with his fairy-like violin. The secret of his punctuality lay in the fact that by the terms of the contract he must forfeit one thousand francs for every non-appearance. The proceeds of my tour in America laid the foundation of my prosperity. On my return I hastened to invest in real estate. I purchased a country residence in Peterhof, and in 1865 I married.[1] My wife has never accompanied me on my travels, and

[1] Rubinstein married Mlle. Vièra Tchékuànov, and has three children, — Jacob, Anna, and Alexander. — TR.

on these occasions I have employed my leisure moments either in reading or in composing. I usually wrote my librettos in German or in French on account of the difficulty of finding Russian librettists, and the consequent delay in putting the opera on the stage. The libretto of "Demon" was written at my request by Viskovàtov, professor at the Dorpat University; that of "Gorùsha" by Dmìtri Avèrkiev.

As to the degree of musical appreciation possessed by the different nations, I believe that Germany stands to-day at the head of the musical world, and this in spite of the fact that she is eaten up with pride in her patriotism, her pietism, and sense of superiority to all other countries. Culture has but slender chance in a nation so absorbed in its bayonets and its unity; but in spite of all these drawbacks it must be confessed that Germany is the most "musical" nation in the world.

The relative knowledge of music among

Germans, French, and English, stated arithmetically, would be somewhat as follows: of the German people at least fifty per cent understand music; of the French not more than sixteen per cent; while among the English — the least musical of people — not more than two per cent can be found who have any knowledge of music. Even the Americans have a higher appreciation of music than the English.

I speak frankly, but without malice, for I have always been most hospitably received in England. . . . But while I am deeply sensible of this kindness to me, I cannot refrain from saying that their ignorance of music is only exceeded by their lack of appreciation. The children of Albion may resent my candor, and perhaps it would have been wiser to have reserved my opinion. . . .

In America we find a little more music than in England. . . . But it is only in Germany that one learns to what noble heights it may attain. In France, music has a special part assigned to it, which is in a prosperous condition and well appreciated; but it is very, very different from Germany. In no other land do we find the real merit of musical compositions so quickly discerned and accurately valued as in Germany. The folk-songs of the Russians stand alone. . . . Only those of Sweden and Norway are worthy to be compared with them for enchanting melody. But I must not say too much in praise of Russian music, lest as a Russian I should be suspected of partisanship.

And now, with the supremacy of Bismarck on the one hand, and Wagnerism on the other, with men's ideals all reversed, dawns the critical moment for music. *Technique* has taken gigantic strides, but composition, to speak frankly, has come to an end. . . . Its parting knell was rung when the last incomparable notes of Chopin died away. It may prove but a temporary paralysis, and who can say how long it may endure ? Between the fifteenth and seventeenth centuries painting stood at the zenith of its power, but during the eighteenth century deterioration set in ; and I believe that music is passing through a similar crisis. . . . When and how it will end no one can know. One thing is beyond denial, — all that enchanted us, all that we loved, respected, worshipped, and admired, has ended with Chopin.

CHAPTER XII.

My articles on music, and my various musical works. — Historical concerts in the principal cities of Europe. — Entrance upon my second term as Director of the Conservatory. — My memoranda and projects. — Reforms in the organization of music in Russia regarded as one of the most effective instruments for popular education.

1852–1889.

RETURNING to the subject of my activity as a writer on music, I remember that in the first number of the " Viek," a periodical started in 1860 by the late Bézobràsov and others, I wrote an article called " Music in Russia " on the subject of dilettanteism in music, violently attacking the dilettanti amateurs, who have wrought only mischief to the cause of music in Russia. . . . The article produced a commotion, and a torrent of abuse descended upon my head; but even now, after the lapse of thirty years, I still adhere to the views advanced at that time. It must be said however that the prevailing dilettanteism against which I had waged war previous to the foundation of the Conservatory has in these days lost its baleful influence, and the article written in 1860 has lost its former significance.

It is but little that I have ever written on the subject of music. Some years ago I wrote an article in German [1] (which was afterward translated into Russian) upon sacred operas or oratorios, and another in the Leipsic magazine "Signal" in answer to a proposition made to me to undertake the editing of a series of musical classics, — an important scheme, whose development would prove a valuable contribution to musical knowledge. Lately I have sketched a plan for drawing up by-laws, accompanied by notes on that subject, and

[1] Rubinstein's letter on the "Geistliche Oper," edited in Berlin in a miscellaneous collection by Lévinski under the title : "Vor den Kullissen."

also on the subject of Russian music in general, which I hope will receive a legal sanction. . . . This is the sum of my activity in that line, and my future biographer will not even enjoy the pleasure of collecting my correspondence, since it has absolutely no existence. I am not a friend to the pen, and especially do I dislike letter-writing.

I have no means of recalling the data of my operas, — that is to say, of their composition; and the date of representation would be of no assistance, because that often took place long after they were written. I remember that "Thomas the Fool" was written in 1852, and the "Demon" in 1871. Several years ago the latter had already been sung over one hundred times, but whether it has been given five times since, I cannot tell. I never addressed the slightest request or even suggestion to the directors concerning my musical works. They may do as they please. I have not the vaguest idea why " Merchant Kalàshnikov " was taken from the *répertoire*. I was greatly pleased to learn that the opera was approved in high quarters, and at the expressed wish of those in authority it was again reinstated; but why, notwithstanding this approval, it was after two or three performances again withdrawn, I cannot possibly imagine. And yet the fact that it paid well, showed that it pleased the public. The " Maccabees," [1] written in 1873-1875, was not performed in St. Petersburg until 1877. My " Nero " was given first in Hamburg. In 1885 I wrote my comic operas " With the Brigands " and " The Parrot."

I cannot claim that my operas have a warm reception at the hands of theatrical managers. Very often when they have

---

[1] When Count **Adlerberg** consented at last to put the " Maccabees " on the stage, he wrote the following order : " It may be given providing that nothing is spent either for costumes or decorations."

been most cordially received outside my native land, our own managers have utterly ignored them. The "Demon" is given very seldom of late years; the "Maccabees," not at all; while "Kalàshnikov" has been withdrawn altogether. . . .

If they are received with favor in the official world, it is only because of influence in high circles. . . . I may be mistaken, but I believe that the secret of the ill-will on the part of the management is not dislike of me personally, but hostility to the Conservatory. . . . I have never spoken a word upon this subject to the directors, who are changed from time to time, and they are always perfectly civil to me. . . . It must be acknowledged that this position of director, not in Russia alone, but in all countries, is by no means to be coveted; and if I were asked if the post of director were not more difficult than that of Minister of Foreign Affairs, I should reply in the affirmative.

The oratorios or the sacred operas of "Paradise Lost" and the "Tower of Babel" were written many years ago, — the former in 1854, and the latter about 1870. The "Moses," a series of musical tableaux, also belongs to this class of composition.

I have written about six symphonies, but most of them have no name. Those best known are the "Ocean," the "Dramatic," and the "Russian." Of the musical tableaux may be mentioned "Iwàn the Terrible," "Don Quixote," and "Faust;" the ballad "Lenore" and the "Eroica," dedicated to the memory of Skòbelev, the manuscript of which I presented to the Bogolùbov museum in Saràtov. Among my earlier works are the musical illustrations to Krylòv's fables: "The Donkey and the Nightingale," "The Cuckoo and the Eagle," "The Grasshopper and the Ant," "The Crow and the Fox," "Parnassus," and "The Quartet;" and among the more recent are the operas "Sulamith" and "Gorùsha." I have set to music a great many of our best poems; but at present I have wholly forgotten both their names and their numbers. They are all enumerated in the catalogues, however.

During the season of 1885–1886 I was able to execute a long cherished plan, and to celebrate the last years of my career as a *virtuoso* by a series of concerts to be given in the chief cities of Europe. These performances were intended to illustrate the gradual development of piano music; lectures on the history of music had been given before, but not historical concerts on the scale that I proposed.

I gave a series of seventeen concerts in each of the following cities: St. Petersburg, Moscow, Vienna, Berlin, London, Paris, and Leipsic; and in some of them every concert that I gave in the evening was repeated the next day for the benefit of the musical students. Both morning and evening concerts were crowded. It was really a great undertaking. I played in St. Petersburg and Moscow alternately, giving two concerts in the one city and then two in the other, until fourteen concerts had been given in each city. I had every reason to be satisfied with the result of these performances, which proved successful in all respects. I suffered no inconvenience either from fatigue of body or mind; my memory served me faithfully. Much of what I played at the concerts I had studied when I was a child. . . . And as to the rest, I spent one summer in studying a good deal of the music that I now played for the first time. I have never employed a prompter; indeed I hardly think that it would be possible to have one. The financial part of the affair was under the management of Wolf, a special agent from Berlin, who received a certain percentage of the profits. I stepped upon the platform with my mind quite free from care or anxiety. This most convenient arrangement has only recently been introduced into Russia. Peterson in St. Petersburg, Jurgenson in Moscow, relieve the artist of every care and responsibility. In regard to Peterson, I will have to mention that he is the sole proprietor of Bekker's piano manufactory, and all rumors to the effect that my savings have been invested in it are without foundation.

Early in the year 1887, I resumed the management of the St. Petersburg Conservatory, and in March of the same year presented a memorial to the Russian Musical Society on the organization of popular theatricals and concerts. The object of this scheme was twofold, — to introduce the works of rising composers, and to give the public a chance to enjoy the talents developed by the Russian conservatories. In the same year I drew up a project for a new constitution for the Conservatory, which was taken under consideration.

The status of music in Russia and the

best possible way of directing musical education, greatly interest me. I have also written a comprehensive memorial on this subject. . . . It is important that our conservatories should be under the administration of the government. The universities, the various academies (the Academy of Fine Arts, for instance), and the higher schools are all under the control of the government, and it should be the same with our conservatories. Individual enterprise and the energy of private societies has effected their organization, but after an existence of thirty years there is no reason why these schools for higher musical education should remain outside the pale of governmental care. The change from private control to that of the government cannot fail to produce the most satisfactory results. Moreover, all other musical schools should be made dependent on the conservatories, and required to furnish a certain contingent of pupils. It would be well to establish conservatories in all the principal centres of Russia, in St. Petersburg, Moscow, Tiflìs, Riga, Warsaw, Kiev, Odessa, and even in Omsk; the more numerous they are, the better. It is still more important that the government maintain at least two conservatories; one in the north of Russia should be for instrumental music, and the other in the south for vocal music. We should consider the advantages of our southern climate for vocal culture and profit by them.

If the Russian government were to assume the superintendence of musical education, — a most important factor in the civilization of its people, — it should, I think, make an effort to establish the opera in the capital of each government.[1] Supported by the material help and moral influence of the government with the cooperation of the governor of each province, as well as that of the local and central

[1] Russia is divided into fifty-two governments. — Tr.

authorities, this would not prove so difficult an undertaking as it might at first appear. There would be no lack of musicians and singers for the conservatories and the musical schools of some of the governments. Khàrkov, Kiev, Saràtov, Tiflìs, and others have already for more than a quarter of a century been engaged in training artists, who only ask for the opportunity to practise the art they have acquired after years of patient study. And with the birth of new conservatories, under the care and direction of the government, the number of musicians will increase, and there will always be a supply ready to meet the demand.

It is an undeniable fact that our provincial society is as much addicted to gambling as our lower classes are to drink, and that ignorance prevails among all orders. One need be no prophet however to foretell the results that will spring from the beneficent influence of a permanent opera in the province. The standard of morality cannot fail to rise, and surely that is a consummation devoutly to be wished, and one which the government in all its public enterprises seeks or should seek to promote. Again the establishment of provincial opera will open a wider field for the rapidly growing contingent of musicians, who are to be trained in these conservatories and music schools. Not until the government takes this matter in hand shall we emerge from the present miserable condition of musical affairs, when Russia supports but two opera troupes; and this can be achieved by government alone. We know too well the result of private enterprise in the provinces,—it almost invariably comes to grief.

It is a well-nigh incredible fact that we have but a single opera troupe in each of the capitals; and how is it possible to be faithful to requirements of national art by giving the works of Russian composers and at the same time to please the public by frequent repetition of foreign operas, as well as ballets? It would require the entire time of one troupe adequately to represent the works of foreign composers of the older schools, excluding those as near to our time as are Mozart and Meyerbeer. All this is not as it should be!

While I am speaking of the provinces, let me suggest that the encouragement of the opera and of popular concerts, together with musical culture in general, should be included in the duties of the governors. And I believe that if the government will but turn its attention to this subject, giving proper directions to the governors, the marshals of nobility, and the mayors, and encourage their efforts, this project cannot fail to succeed. In a monarchical country like ours, where both *régime* and governmental authority are very strong, where it is not only the right of that country, but its sacred duty to care for and to guide the masses, it can hardly fail, I think, to give its serious consideration to the establishment and development of musical training.

And futhermore, I would urge that classes in music be formed in every educational institution to whatsoever grade it may belong, not merely to teach the boys and girls to sing songs or church music, but to give them solid instruction in the fundamental principles of music. Look at Germany and America, and see how they do things in those countries. . . . I demand no useless innovations; I do not ask for children's orchestras, like one I saw in a school in St. Petersburg, for that takes too much of the children's time; but let the first elements of music be taught in all schools as one of the regular studies, so that every boy and girl may have learned the alphabet of music while yet in school. Believe me, this will bring forth a rich harvest. The conservatories must maintain a high standard; and the right to grant diplomas, such as are given after a close examination by the universities and other special schools, should be restricted to them alone. That is the only method by which this matter of diplomas can be properly controlled. Every instructor in the different branches of music should be required to show a certificate from the conservatories, granting the right to teach music in families and schools, similar to those required from every tutor and governess who teaches the common branches, either in schools or in private families. In regard to the theatre, I do not hold with those who would cater to the popular taste by representing the works of second-rate dramatists. It would be far better to give those of Pùshkin, Gògol, Goethe, Shakspeare, and other great writers, both native and foreign. Let us not minister to the cravings of the ignorant for foolish amusement; what satisfaction can there be for a *mujik* to pay even fifteen kopecks to see on the stage the same drunkard in sheepskin whom he meets in the pothouse? If the theatre is to be a medium of education, let it be above the people. It may be that at first the lower classes will find such pieces dull and uninteresting; but believe me, it will not be long before they will have learned to appreciate their beauties, and will seek the theatre, now become an instrument of civilization for the masses. Much has been written and spoken on this subject, but few care to consider in earnest the importance of the matter, and are still less willing to do their part toward promoting its realization.

Between 1860 and 1870 much has been accomplished in the direction of reform in the methods of musical education in Russia. Very little had been done for music before that time; and in spite of the genius of Glinka, Russian opera was held in disfavor. Since the establishment of the Russian Musical Society and the Conservatory, a network of musical societies and music schools has gradually covered the land. Thus the government has already on hand not only a large amount of musical material, but establishments for its further production; and all that remains now is to consider the musical development of Russia a State affair, and to place conservatories and musical schools in the Bureau of Public Instruction, on the same footing with universities and gymnasiums.

I make these few cursory remarks by the way, but all my ideas concerning the proper conditions of musical establishments and musical education in Russia, and what should be done to promote their prosperity, I have set down systematically and in detail in a separate memorial.

I firmly believe that in view of the deep interest felt by the highest authorities in this noble problem of civilization, — the liberation of the masses from the slough of vice, and the opening out to them of a means of moral development through the medium of the arts,— many of my projects will be adopted, and ways will be provided to carry them into execution for the benefit of our beloved country and the welfare of many millions of the Russian people.

May God grant this! As for myself, the ideas which I have striven to express are confirmed by many years of experience and a thorough acquaintance with the subject in question; and I can truly affirm that my sole motive has been to serve my dear native land according to the best of my knowledge and ability.

ANTON RUBINSTEIN.

St. Petersburg,
  October, 1889.

SUPPLEMENT.

RUBINSTEIN AS A COMPOSER.

IT is too soon to speak of Rubinstein as a composer; he is not even an old man, and his talent is in full vigor. No doubt he will yet give us many works. The future alone can determine which of them will go down to posterity, to be cherished as precious pearls in musical literature. Even now, however, the characteristic features of the famous master's compositions are sufficiently defined to enable us to determine with more or less accuracy the rank which this or that noted work occupies in the musical literature of the present day.

While yet in his early childhood, Rubinstein developed the gift of composition. His artistic nature endowed with a remarkably imaginative feeling for melody, and a wealth of invention, manifested itself at every turn. Hardly a musical form escaped him, and there are but few of which he has not given us some fine examples. Many a day when overborne by hard work and engrossing outside occupations, he would seize an hour to devote to his favorite occupation of composing. And now that he is not diverted from it, he gives himself up to it almost exclusively.

If we cast a glance at the catalogue of Rubinstein's compositions we shall be no less surprised at the number of them than at the versatility of his genius. It includes five symphonies, five concertos for the piano, several overtures, trios and quartets, thirteen operas, two oratorios, and many songs. Only one richly endowed with the gift of melody could have produced them all.

Rubinstein's melodies are for the most part original, although sometimes the influence of Mendelssohn may be felt; but the majority of them, as in the "Maccabees," the "Demon," the "Tower of Babel," are of an Oriental character. This is true, however, of all Russian music. Some of his *motifs* have the general character of European music and often remind one of Mendelssohn, which is not to be wondered at when we remember that in his youth Rubinstein was under the influence of the Mendelssohnian school; for it is an acknowledged fact that even the greatest composers have felt the influence of their predecessors.

In regard to the forms which Rubinstein uses, they are exclusively old classical, and have nothing whatever in common with Berlioz, Wagner, or Liszt. By thus persistently ignoring the progress of operatic and dramatic music, the compositions of Rubinstein have certainly gained nothing.

The "Battle of Kulikòvo," his first "test opera," if we may so call it, which met with a certain success, was written in 1850. This was followed in 1853 by the one-act opera of "The Siberian Huntsmen" and "Thomas the Fool;" the latter was given but once, and at his own request withdrawn from the stage. A three-act ballet called "The Grape-Vine" was never given on any stage. "The Children of the Steppes," written in 1860 or thereabout, met with no favor when it was presented in Moscow; and in the opera of "Vengeance," written in 1853, the bacchanalian song of Zulima, "Pour to the brim the noble juice," alone survives. His lyric opera "Feramors," based on the Oriental theme of Moore's "Lalla Rookh," received some notice. Rubinstein is particularly devoted to Oriental *motifs*, and in such he achieves his greatest triumphs. The "Dances of the Bayaderes" from this opera, and the aria "I am oppressed," have won such popularity that they are often to be found on concert programmes. This opera, although popular abroad, was not a favorite in Russia. His best and most familiar opera is undoubtedly the "Demon," written in 1871, and given both in St. Petersburg and Moscow more than one hundred times. Its first performance took place in St. Petersburg on January 13, 1873, for the benefit of the barytone Mêlnikov. Here again the best portions of the opera are those in which the author uses Oriental *motifs*, — such as the "Scene of the Caravan," the "Dance of the Women" and the "Lezghinka."[1] This opera was a grand success both at home and abroad; it was followed by the "Maccabees," the plot of which is taken from the Bible, and in which the Greek and Hebrew elements are manifested by two distinct styles. The distinguishing characteristic of this opera is that the plot is not founded on love, but on the struggle of two nationalities for religion and indepen-

[1] Circassian dance.

dence. It greatly resembles an oratorio, and has been given many times both in Russia and abroad. Berensdorf, musical critic of Leipsic, says that in it Rubinstein has stated and solved the whole problem, and that this music is remarkable for its brilliant coloring, its wealth of imagination, and its inspiration.

Then came "Nero" and "Merchant Kalàshnikov." "Nero" is written on Barbié's libretto, and is in four acts with eight tableaux. It was composed for the Paris *Grand Opèra*, and was sung in Italian in Russia. It is unnecessarily long, and crowded with useless details that hamper the action; the characters are numerous, and many of them have very difficult *rôles*. The greater part of the opera consists of recitatives in which Rubinstein is by no means at his best. We miss the Oriental element; still it has many fine passages, the finest of which is the tableau in the fourth act, where Nero is haunted by the shades of his murdered victims. "Nero" is no longer included in the *répertoire*.

"Merchant Kalàshnikov" is written on Lèrmontov's epic poem entitled "Song about the Czar Ivàn Vassìlievich, the young *Oprichnik*,[1] and the gallant merchant Kalàshnikov." It is in three acts with four tableaux, and was put on the stage under the direction of the composer, and received with crowded houses in St. Petersburg on January 22 and February 25, 1880, but for some reason unknown to the general public was almost immediately withdrawn from the *répertoire*. Those who heard it, speak of it with enthusiasm, as of an opera possessing remarkable merit. Here the *motifs* are based upon Russian folk-song, and the characters are eminently Russian.

[1] Body-guard of the czars, who rebelled at the accession of Peter the Great, and were by him suppressed altogether.

Rubinstein had before now, in the "Battle of Kulikòvo" and in "Thomas the Fool," attempted to introduce the national element into his operas, without much success. But the character of Merchant Kalàshnikov was a perfect success. By this opera he proved his ability to write Russian as well as Oriental and German music, and showed that he was not to be excluded from the ranks of Russian composers. "Merchant Kalàshnikov" has no prominent female *rôle*; the part of Aliëna is purely subordinate, as it should be, to give a correct idea of the position of woman in the times of the *Domostròi*.[1] The dramatic interest rising steadily to a climax forms one of its chief merits. The last act, — the execution of the hero and his farewell to his family, — produces a profound and striking impression. All the characters, that of the *oprìchnik* Kiribèievich, Kalàshnikov, Nikìtka the fool, the gossiping

[1] The old code of Russian sumptuary laws.

Solomonìda, the Tartar Chulubèi, and the Czar Ivàn, are powerfully and sincerely drawn. Aliëna's part is not so well sustained; her aria, "I will enter the sacred temple," in spite of its musical beauty is wholly devoid of national coloring. The choruses are a prominent feature of the opera. The chorus of the *Oprìchniks* in the first act, written in the ecclesiastical style, is very impressive. The female chorus of neighbors is lively and realistic. Those at the meeting of the Czar on the Moscow river, and that of the execution of Merchant Kalàshnikov, are also worthy of mention; the latter is accompanied by the ringing of bells. The dances of the jesters, and Nikìtka's song, "There lived an eagle in a distant land," are also fine. In "Merchant Kalàshnikov" as well as in the "Maccabees" we find Rubinstein's orchestration somewhat monotonous; but in the former there are fortunately no recitatives. Among the solos we may mention

Kalàshnikov's aria, "They have stolen the bird from the nest;" the aria of Kiribèievich in the first act, "Oh, our sovereign Ivàn Vassilievich;" and also Kalàshnikov's duet with Aliëna, "Where hast thou been, wife" etc. On the whole, the opera has many pages of genuine inspiration, and might have become as great a favorite as the "Demon" if it had not been unfortunately withdrawn from the *répertoire*.

His last two comic operas, "With the Brigands" and "The Parrot," as well as the biblical opera "Sulamith," were published in Germany.

In his operatic works, Rubinstein manifests a disposition to follow his own inspiration regardless of the laws laid down by this school or that, and in none of his compositions is the peculiarity more marked than in his symphonic music. Few of his symphonies are preceded by the usual explanatory programme of modern composers. Brought up on German music, he follows in the footprints of Beethoven.

Rubinstein has written five symphonies; the Second is called the "Ocean," the Fourth the "Dramatic;" the others have no titles. The Ocean Symphony was written many years ago and from that time his renown as a composer was established. It is one of his principal works. It was originally written in four parts, but the author afterward added two movements, — the second *adagio* and the second *scherzo*. The musical critic Ambros in comparing it to Beethoven's Pastoral Symphony, likens the "Sailor's Dance" (the first *scherzo*) to the "Peasant's Merry-making," and the final *choral* to the "Glad and grateful feelings after the storm" in the "Pastoral." Ambros alluded to the discretion which Rubinstein showed in leaving the storm to the imagination of the hearers. Afterward, however, and as if by intention, a seventh movement was added.

called "The Storm," in which Rubinstein gave evidence of his thorough knowledge of *technique*.

The Fourth Symphony, in D minor, may also be included among his best work, and occupies a prominent place in musical literature. In the beginning of the decade of 1870 Rubinstein made a prolonged and exhaustive tour of Germany, giving this symphony to admiring audiences. It is rich in *motifs* and masterly in orchestration. The composer introduces the instruments separately, like characters in an opera. It contains long monologues, dialogues, etc; hence its title "Dramatic." The introduction to the first movement is very picturesque; the *scherzo* of the second, written after the manner of Beethoven, animated and full of life, offers a distinct contrast to the emotional *adagio* that follows it. The final movement is rich in color, although somewhat long in comparison with the preceding movements.

The Third Symphony has been less frequently heard in the concert room. The *adagio* and the *scherzo* of this symphony have been much admired for their beautiful *motif* and fine instrumentation.

The Fifth, the so-called "Russian Symphony," has never won the popular favor. It is founded exclusively on Russian melodies, and breathes the very spirit of the country. The *allegro* with its characteristic Russian dance, performed on wooden instruments, is very spirited; the *andante* is rather long, and the melodies played by the horns are uninteresting and monotonous.

Rubinstein has also written a quantity of concertos and chamber music, including three characteristic musical portraits, "Don Quixote," "Ivàn the Terrible," and "Faust."

The famous orchestral portrait of "Don Quixote" may be reckoned among his most successful works. The argument is as follows: —

"The reading of chivalric romances exalting the exploits of knights errant in service of fair ladies and in aid of the oppressed in general, excite in Don Quixote a desire to imitate their example; whereupon he dons the helmet and coat of mail, and sets forth on his bony steed Rosinante. His first encounter is with a flock of sheep, whom he disperses, and encouraged by the success of this exploit pursues his journey. A little farther on he meets three peasant women singing cheerfully at their work, one of whom he selects for the lady of his love, — his Dulcinea. He declares his passion, and vows to perform all his future deeds of prowess in her honor. The peasant women, taking him for a madman, laugh in his face and run away. Don Quixote seems perplexed; but still hoping to win renown by his future exploits he goes on his way. He next falls in with a band of criminals being led to execution, whom he takes for the innocent victims of despotism, and straightway determines to set them free. He attacks the guards and puts them to flight, but in the course of a discussion into which he enters with the liberated criminals he irritates them; they fall on him, and give him a sound drubbing. Here follows the worthy knight's despair. He sees his folly, and dies."

Such are the incidents which Rubinstein has selected for his musical portraiture. He has illustrated only the humorous side of Don Quixote's career; the fundamental conception of the romance,— that Don Quixote is a man of lofty ideals, ready to die for truth and justice, — does not lend itself to music, and Rubinstein has chosen only detached incidents, such as may be described by music. He handles this theme in his usual masterly manner. All in it is essential, nothing superfluous. The work has been arranged for four hands by Tchaikòvski.

The second musical portrait, "Ivàn the Terrible," was performed at a concert in Smolènsk on the 20th of May 1885, on the occasion of the unveiling of Glìnka's monument. The first *allegro* describes the wild orgies of the *Oprichniks,* the Czar's wrath, his repentence and prayer, the groans of the suffering. In vivid colors the composer depicts the sentiments aroused by the contemplation of that period. It is one of Rubinstein's best works on a Russian theme.

"Faust" is the third musical portrait. In treating this subject Rubinstein seems to have been attracted by the lyric side of the tragedy; it is therefore free from the confusion and discord which other composers have employed in depicting Faust's state of mind and the aspect of Mephistopheles. A quartet of strings plays the chief part in a smoothly flowing harmonious discourse.

Among Rubinstein's most important orchestral works "Russia" and the "Eroica" may be included.

"Russia" was written on the occasion of the opening of the Russian Exposition of the Arts and Trades, and offers a mechanical combination of *motifs* representing the various nationalities that people that vast country.

The " Eroica " is said to have been written on the death of Skòbelev. Both these works show signs of haste, with little or no inspiration. The counterpoint development of the themes, however, is extremely interesting.

Glancing rapidly over Rubinstein's chamber and concert music, we will mention only a few of the more important works. It is a department in which he has shown himself prolific. Here we may find octets, sextets, quintets, trios, and concertos for the piano, violin, violoncello, etc.

The G minor quintet. — In this quintet the score for the piano predominates. It opens with an introduction suggestive of the theme of the *allegro* $\frac{3}{4}$ that follows, — a theme which deepens to pathos in the next *motif*, constructed on a simple minor triad. Its simplicity positively amazes the listener. In the second movement the *scherzo* has a *motif* of a Russian type, quite original and graphic; the third movement, an *adagio*, resembles the music of the Greek Church; the *finale* somewhat wearies the listener by its long-drawn thematical development, but we also meet many new melodies, only one of which has a national character. As we have before stated, Rubinstein was brought up on the German classics, and rarely uses Russian melodies; they seem to have had no influence whatever upon the character of his compositions and to have interested him only from a musical point of view.

Rubinstein wrote five trios, two of which — one in F major and the other in G minor, written long before the others, when he was under the influence of Mendelssohn — are extremely interesting. Von Bulow's statement that Rubinstein's style is not unlike that of Beethoven is correct as regards the

B major trio, although even here the imitation of Mendelssohn is evident. In this trio the *andante* shows intense dramatic power.

Rubinstein wrote five concertos for the piano; the majority of his concertos require from the performer a perfect *technique*, and a knowledge of the effects which may be produced on the instrument. All his concertos have an intrinsic meaning, and the significance of the theme is skilfully worked out.

To this class belongs the "Caprice Russe," dedicated to the famous pianist Madame Èssipov. It is a *fantaisie* on various Russian songs, with an orchestral accompaniment. The *motifs* of this *fantaisie* are delicately worked out. After several variations played by the orchestra on a slow and rhythmical Russian melody, the piano takes up the same air with all the intervals reversed. This method in counterpoint gives us a charming new melody, which comes in at the end of this movement in the major key and forms the last *motif*, for which the composer makes a delightful accompaniment on the piano, using it at the same time by the way of transition to the next triumphal song. This song is played by the orchestra with a brilliant accompaniment of piano, after which the first slow air reappears in the piano score, while at the same time we hear from the orchestra a third merry dance-song, upon which the whole *finale* is constructed, bringing in the three melodies simultaneously.

We will but touch upon Rubinstein's lesser piano works, most of which contain interesting musical conceptions, and are known under the name of "Miscellaneous." Opus 93, composed of nine numbers, deserves special mention.

No. 1. The Ballad of Lenore. — This work belongs to the programme music. It was written on the theme of Bürger's famous ballad. Lenore awaits the return of her betrothed from the war. Peace is concluded, and the troops come marching home with beating of drums and martial music. Vainly she looks for the face of her loved one; he has perished in the battle. Deaf to the words of her mother, who strives to comfort her, Lenore curses her fate. That night a trooper appears to her, bids her to follow him and share his home, — the grave. All night they gallop over hill and vale, till they come to the graveyard. Rubinstein illustrates this theme with picturesque details; we feel Lenore's sadness, we hear the military march of the returning troops, and the mad galloping of the rider with his beloved.

No. 2. Variations on an American national air. — This work consists of an introduction and a theme with thirty-nine variations, followed by a *Dùmka*[1] and a *Polonaise* (dedicated to Mademoiselle Tèr-

[1] "*Dùmka*" is a *genre* of Ruthenian song.

minski),[1] the first of which is tinged with a deep melancholy.

No. 4 contains two Russian serenades, studies, a *scherzo*, a *barcarolle*, and two *morceaux* (Nos. 5, 6, 7, 8), all specimens of an attractive style of music. The last number, " Miniatures," consists of twelve pieces, the more prominent of which are, " At the Brook," " Serenade," " Oriental March," and " Cradle Song." In this class may be included the popular " Valse Caprice," which has achieved an immense success.

We may likewise mention his " Bal Costumé," several numbers of which have been arranged for the orchestra by Ermansdörfer. It consists of twenty numbers, and is remarkable for the brilliancy of coloring with which the different nationalities are indicated. We must not forget to mention his concertos for violin and violoncello, for they help to supplement the

[1] A well-known Russian pianist.

rather scanty contributions to this class of musical literature. The A minor violin sonata, Opus 19, is rich in musical effects.

He has also written a great many songs.

RUBINSTEIN AS A PIANIST.

WE must devote a brief space to the consideration of Rubinstein as a pianist.

His first appearance on the concert platform is contemporary with the birth of musical criticism. There can be no simpler means of introducing the reader to the characteristics of Rubinstein as a pianist, than to quote the opinions of several well-known musical critics.

This is what Brachvogel has written concerning him : —

"No artist has ever before shown to his audience so merciless a front. Both his programmes and his attitude are absolutely uncompromising. At first sight one is conscious of something stern, even inimical in his bearing toward his audience, as though a chasm were fixed between them, and he stood ready to plunge single-handed into the conflict; but gradually the sense of hostility vanishes, and the great artist conquers once and forever. Rubinstein has no idea of descending to the level of popular taste, he can only raise his audience to his own plane. It is enough to look in his face to understand what it all means. He has the head of an inspired sphinx, upon whose face not even the paroxysms of enthusiasm call forth a smile. Did not the color of life illumine it, it might be of stone. Those who have heard his playing will never forget it."

Hanslick thus characterizes Rubinstein's playing: —

"We always follow Rubinstein's playing with a sense of infinite delight. His youthful and untiring vigor, his incomparable power of bringing out the melody, his perfection of touch in the stormy torrents of passion, as well as in the tender long-drawn notes of pathos, his wonderful memory, and his energy that knows no fatigue, — these are the qualities which amaze us in Rubinstein's playing. His rendering of Chopin's B minor Sonata is indeed wonderful; he plays the first movement tempestuously, giving to it the atmosphere of passionate gloom; the funeral march is stern and sustained; the mighty *crescendo* at the beginning of the trio, and the gradual *decrescendo* after it, is a brilliant innovation of his own. But in the *finale* he takes such an astounding *prestissimo* that all accents are lost, and only a gray cloud of dust seems to hover before the dazed listener, who simply waits for the last note that he may open his eyes and draw a long breath of relief. Therefore young *virtuosi* must beware of imitating the excesses of Rubinstein's playing, rather learning from him to play with expression, keeping all the while strict watch over the *tempo*. The sentimental fluctuations of the measure by which young pianists, and lady pianists in particular, disfigure the noblest inspirations of Chopin, is unendurable to Rubinstein. One finds no vestige of this caricature of *tempo rubato*, or any affectation whatsoever in Rubinstein's playing. It is a delight to listen to him, in the highest and most sincere sense of the word. A vigorous and wholesome current of feeling flows so refreshingly over the hearer that he receives the impression of having been in a musical symposium, to the unspeakable delectation of his ear.

"The merits of Rubinstein's playing are sought principally in his elementary power, and from this same source spring likewise many of his faults. With years, however, his playing has become more equal. The bewitching beauty of his tones, the power and delicacy of his touch have now reached their climax. One seldom finds in contemporary pianists that genuine, spontaneous inward fervor which in the heat of passion dares all things, even to indiscretion, rather than pause to reason and reflect. Where reflection is absent there may be heard the overwhelming voice of the passions and the heart-strings echoing in response. Rubinstein's temperament is of such compelling force that exhausted Europe yields submission to his will."

The following is taken from the criticism of the well-known Russian critic Levensohn, who wrote it a few years ago under the immediate influence of Rubinstein's concerts in Moscow: —

"Many years ago the famous historian Thomas Carlyle, in his lecture on 'Hero-Worship,' says in effect: Nothing so elevates mankind as the worship of men of genius. However much the eternal cavillers may strive to pick flaws, the enthusiasm of those who have truly learned to love great men with all the strength of their souls will suffer no loss. This is the kind of feeling inspired by Rubinstein. Can there be a higher delight for the man who loves and appreciates music than to see and hear the man of genius? In listening to Anton Rubinstein, one receives an impression not unlike that produced by some magnificent display of the elements. His creations at the piano are as spontaneous as those of Nature herself, and this is the secret of his personal influence. His *répertoire* embraces the entire range of compositions, beginning with the works of

Handel and ending with his own. His passionate temperament often carries him beyond the lawful boundaries; for instance, he takes too rapid a *tempo* in the *prestissimo* of Beethoven's Sonata, Op. 109, hindering the listener from following in detail this desperate soul-shriek; he also plays Chopin's F major Ballad too rapidly. On the other hand, the beauty of certain compositions is never fully appreciated until we hear them interpreted by Rubinstein. Thus in Chopin's Nocturne, Op. 37, the heart-rending wail is interrupted by a succession of Palestrina-like chords. In Rubinstein's rendering, it is as if these chords were played on the organ. We feel, however, that these religious strains fail to soothe the suffering soul. The desperate cry is renewed and grief resumes its sway. This soul-picture of a lonely sufferer, who seeks consolation in religion and fails to find it, — such is the theme of this nocturne, which becomes intelligible in Rubinstein's rendering. For another example take the last variation in Beethoven's Sonata, Op. 109, with that never ending trill, which passes through several octaves; you feel yourself in the presence of a sphinx. But lo! beneath the fingers of Rubinstein this labyrinth of sounds becomes an almost indistinguishable murmur, and through this murmur, penetrating it like a sunbeam, comes the E major theme; then you see the necessity of the preceding chaos.

"From out the numberless proofs of genius of which his playing gives evidence, we will select his rendering of Handel's theme, with its beaded ornamentations (known in the old times under the name of *agréments*), the second variation of this air executed by octaves in the bass, and the wonderful transition from the lower to the higher register in the second theme of Beethoven's C major Sonata, Op. 53; indeed the grandeur of his rendering of that sonata cannot be too highly praised. His daintiness of execution in Schumann's 'Traumes-Wirren' and 'Vogel als Prophet,' as well as the 'singing' of the second theme in Chopin's B minor *scherzo*, reminds one of his own far-away childhood and the happy days of youth, now gone forever, that visited us ere we plunged into the turmoil of life. Were we to recall all the moments wherein Rubinstein stirs the soul of his hearer, we should never have done.

"Why allude to the *technique* of this man of genius? Here also he differs from all others, and sets at defiance formerly accepted methods. How is one to play the rapid octave accompaniment of the Schubert-Liszt 'Erl König'? Any professor will tell you to do it with a light wrist, and the middle fingers extended. And what does Rubinstein do? He curves the middle fingers and raises the wrist, so that the fingers that play the octaves instead of falling sideways on the keys strike with their tips as with a hammer. By this method the octaves are played with ease and freedom, whereas in the rendering of other pianists one is always sensible of the effort. There is no living pianist who could imitate him in this. It is his own invention and a manner peculiar to himself. An Oriental on meeting a man of genius says a special prayer for the occasion. We too have our own way of expressing our enthusiasm. One can realize the excitement of the public at each appearance of Rubinstein only in witnessing it."

In January 1889 Rubinstein played in Moscow for the last time; and as he came upon the stage at the close of the performance to make his final bow of acknowledgement, the lid of the grand piano was locked. He made one pathetic gesture of farewell, and disappeared from the concert-room forever.

THE END.